CW01663170

MMM5

Modern Music Masters – The Verve

Richard Bowes

Modern Music Masters

ISBN: 978-1-8381887-4-0
modernmusicmastersuk@gmail.com

DEDICATION

This book is dedicated to fans of The Verve everywhere, and to Debbie for her excellent colour choices.

CONTENTS

ACKNOWLEDGMENTS

Thank you to all the following, without whom this book would not have been possible:

Thank you to Tom Boniface-Webb for entrusting me to contribute to his series, my thanks go to him for the commission and the trust he has shown in me.
Cover Design: Barry Parkinson at www.beepea.co.uk
www.discogs.com
Special thanks to the UK Official Charts Company, the most invaluable resource for this book series
Series editor: Tom Boniface-Webb

Books in the Modern Music Masters Series:

Oasis
Blur
Pulp
Manic Street Preachers
The Verve
Suede

MMM5 – The Verve Spotify Playlist

Available at: MMM5 – The Verve

FOREWORD:

I have always loved The Verve, being just as obsessed with the blissed-out space jams of Gravity Grave as much as the moody indie-rock of History, and was one of the assembled masses who waited with bated breath for the release of *Urban Hymns*, just as I started the sixth form, in September 1997. So I'm thrilled to be adding their incredible story to the *Modern Music Masters* series.

The Verve are from the classic mould of rock 'n' roll bands. Led by the extravert singer Richard Ashcroft, a man just as much at home dancing on the mixing desk, or on stage at Glastonbury, as he is strumming a heartfelt ballad on an acoustic guitar in a studio control room. He is joined by the genius yet tricky guitarist with mystique (quote – *Almost Famous*), Nick McCabe, his key creative foil, and they are backed by one of the most solid yet inventive rhythm sections in British indie-rock, Simon Jones and Pete Salisbury. They are from a Northern English city yet have much to say about the world, and their songs are about a myriad of things, with meanings at once cosmic yet intimate, none of them being about football or drinking.

Watching their success grow throughout the late nineties felt exonerating, none more so than for the band themselves. Since they first came to prominence with singles like Slide Away and She's a Superstar in 1992, it felt like they were just one step away from greatness, if they could just put their finger on it, and keep those arguments – which so many bands are prone to, but seemed to effect The Verve more than most – out of the studio long enough to grab it. Bittersweet Symphony, despite its legal wranglings, will go down in history as one of the all-time great British indie anthems, and no-one can take that away from them. But that's enough from me, I'll let Richard tell their story.

Welcome to *Modern Music Masters – The Verve*, the fifth entry in the growing series, and the second book not to be written by me. The series is incredibly lucky to have bagged a writer of Richard Bowes' talent, and, suitably enough, I first became aware of his work whilst researching the first of the MMM series, Oasis, on whom he has written the definitive biography, *Some Might Say*, published by This Day in Music Books, in 2020.

Richard has chosen his subject well, because there are seemingly few other books on the band, in comparison to many of their contemporaries. As he mentions in his introduction, there is *The Verve: Star Sail*, and *Richard Ashcroft: The Verve, Burning Money & The Human Condition*, and I would throw into that mix the 1998 biography, *The Verve: Crazed Highs and Horrible Lows*, by Martin Clarke, published by Plexus Publishing, although it was probably released a little too early to offer any real insight into their impact on British music. Although, I would of course recommend Richard's book over any of them, and I think you've done the right thing in reading it.

As always, we hope you enjoy the journey, and don't forget to let us know what you think. And also, make sure to tune in for news on upcoming editions to the growing *Modern Music Masters* family.

Tom Boniface-Webb
March 2021

A FEW WORDS FROM THE AUTHOR

I was a late comer to The Verve, but hopefully you will forgive me; I was 10 years of age when they released their first single and nearly 12 by the time their debut album was unveiled. Hardly the target audience, I'm sure you'll agree.

My first recollection of The Verve is of seeing the video to This Is Music when it was on ITV's *The Chart Show*. I remember being taken aback of the shot of the lift door opening to reveal Richard Ashcroft, but the song didn't resonate with me. Of course, I now appreciate that it ranks as one of their best songs, with its genius being its lack of accessibility. As a mad Oasis fan, hoovering up every bit of Gallagher-related content I could find, I was aware of this 'bunch of space cadets' Noel Gallagher would often refer to, and my interest was piqued by the dedication to Ashcroft on the sleeve notes of *(What's The Story) Morning Glory?* I listened to *A Northern Soul* and, although History and On Your Own spoke to my pop-attuned ears, I was still too young to fully appreciate what an astonishing piece of work it is. Also, by the time …*Morning Glory* was released The Verve had split up so, to me, there seemed little point investigating further. Why listen to 'old' music when there was so much great 'new' music to be focussed on?

Then Bitter Sweet Symphony happened. The world changed and I, like thousands of other music fans, experienced an almighty wake-up call. I consumed *Urban Hymns* daily, drinking in its secrets as the band took over the world for a brief spell and then, once *Urban Hymns* and the B-sides were exhausted, I went through their back catalogue with new ears. My friends and I were so inspired that, despite living in Reading, we decided to trawl all the way to Chelmsford, Essex for our first ever festival experience (V98) just so we could see The Verve in the flesh. We were fortunate, as they split up some weeks later, but I have been a fully paid-up member of the faithful ever since, buying Richard Ashcroft's singles long after my friends had abandoned him.

The first phase of Richard Ashcroft's solo career contained some highs that were nearly comparable to his work with The Verve. Nearly. The Shining's one and only album (*True Skies*) was virtually all we heard from the rest of the band until the reunion of 2007. Of all the reunions before and since, none have meant quite so much, with the possible exception of The Stone Roses. I am very aware I'm in the minority here, but I feel that Love Is Noise ranks as one of The Verve's very best songs and was therefore worth the reunion alone. *Forth* may not quite match up to their first three albums but, as Ashcroft himself said, it is still better than most other bands' efforts. Fortunately, now we have easy access to most recorded music via streaming and downloading platforms, it is much easier to keep track of the careers of Nick McCabe and Simon Jones. Their work since The Verve's last split in 2009 has been a good counterpoint to Ashcroft's and, while it is no substitute for the glory of them playing together, it is great to see them releasing music after a quiet spell in the early part of this century.

The overall focus for the *Modern Music Masters* series is to view the individual subject matter through the prism of the charts. Given that they only released a total of 14 singles across their four albums, I have decided to delve deeper into the mechanics and activities of the band across their career. Since embarking on his solo career, Richard Ashcroft has released more music than The Verve (more or less) and would arguably be a better candidate for chart evaluation but, in the nicest possible way, the story of his previous band is far more interesting.

While researching for this book, I have discovered a wealth of new information that I was not aware of. For that reason, I owe a huge debt of gratitude to two books: *The Verve: Star* Sail by Sean Egan (Omnibus Press, 1998) and *Richard Ashcroft: The Verve, Burning Money & The Human Condition* by Trevor Baker (Independent Music Press, 2008). I make no claims that this book goes into anywhere near the detail of those two works. I stand on the shoulders of giants, and thoroughly recommend them both for deeper dives into The Verve. I would also like to acknowledge the debt of gratitude I owe to www.theverveonline.com , www.thevervelive.com , www.richardashcroftonline.com and www.officialcharts.com . Invaluable resources all.

Despite their acclaim and success, I believe The Verve are one of the most underrated bands of the 1990s. This book is my attempt to go some way to validating that claim.

n.b. all songs written by Ashcroft/Jones/McCabe/Salisbury, unless otherwise stated.

CHAPTER ONE
'Walking With a Man Called Sun, I Think my Journey's Just Begun' (1988-1991)

Despite its proximity to the two hotbeds of North-West culture (Liverpool & Manchester), the town of Wigan can easily lay claim to some key cultural contributions. George Formby Jnr was once the UK's highest-paid entertainer and, following in the footsteps of his father, cultivated an act that amused audiences across the globe. In the 1970s, the Wigan Casino was the authority on Northern Soul nights, with youngsters across the country flocking to its infamous discotheque. Although it didn't do much to enhance the town's reputation for poverty, very few towns can claim to have had a whole book dedicated to them as George Orwell's *The Road to Wigan Pier* was in 1937. In sport, the Wigan Warriors have dominated rugby league since their inception in 1872, and the football team has had some success in the 21st century.

Despite a cultural history to be proud of, Wigan hasn't been known as a thriving area for British music. Even less so in the late 1980s. The four young men who were to soon become an entity known as Verve began operating in the same orbit at Winstanley Sixth Form College in Billinge, east Wigan. Richard Ashcroft, a young man studying theatre, philosophy, and English, claims to have heard some guitar sounds emanate from a practice room in 1989, and later described the sound as 'like a whole other universe to me'. The relationship and aspirations between Richard Ashcroft and Nick McCabe blossomed from there. Simon Jones soon joined the pair as did Pete Salisbury, both known to Ashcroft from their days at Up Holland High school. All four Verve members tried their hands, unsuccessfully, at various bands but never all at the same time. Also operating in the vicinity was one Simon Tong. More on him later.

According to the sleeve notes in the deluxe boxset of *A Storm in Heaven*, McCabe was already in a band with a female singer whose services were quickly dispensed with upon his laying eyes on Richard Ashcroft. Describing himself as part of 'the nerd set' in comparison to Ashcroft (earmarked as one of the more popular kids), it would appear on the surface that common ground would be sparse between the pair, but McCabe states that the opposite is true, the duo complementing each other rather than alienating, bonding over channelling their individual anxieties into something more positive.

For a spell, Ashcroft and McCabe operated under two names: The Butterfly Effect and Raingarden, both of which were guitar-heavy (with McCabe finding his feet sonically) and had their first-ever live performances at the canteen of Winstanley. Ashcroft was said to be an uninhibited performer, at one point throwing himself to the floor and rolling around frantically, a style which would eventually lead to him being dubbed 'Mad Richard' by the music press. Ashcroft has often claimed that he gets lost in the music (which is also very apparent to those watching) but had perhaps yet to find his methodology, though the seeds of his embracing the sounds surrounding him were very obviously sown. Another, more mundane, version of the story states that Ashcroft was introduced to the other members by a mutual friend Liam Begley. As would become his trademark, when telling the story, the singer made poetry out of the mundane.

Simon Jones claims that Nick and Richard's band was more electronically influenced than others at Winstanley, with McCabe programming a drum machine that would allow him to also play guitar. For reasons unknown, Ashcroft parted ways with McCabe and joined a band with Jones for a short period as McCabe, a year older, left the college. After the guitarist agreed to join a new project with Ashcroft and Jones, three-quarters of the original Verve line-up was in place.

Richard Ashcroft's mother had recently remarried (after the death of Ashcroft's father when he was 11) and moved with her new husband to Stroud, some 150 miles away, leaving her son to stay with a friend(s), an ideal location (namely with no parents) to rehearse for the burgeoning musicians. The trio took their time in working each other out; Jones and McCabe initially both played guitar but, upon seeing the latter's dexterity and expression come out through his instrument, the former opted to play bass in the knowledge that he would not be able to compete with the senior guitarist, nor would he be prepared to consider it.

McCabe was curious about creating sounds on the guitar rather than just chords, with Jones noting that he had a surplus of equipment just to play one instrument. Synthesizers and drum machines were among the plethora of toys at the guitarist's flat in Haydock. McCabe was a musical adventurer, varying his palate with difficult leftfield music and more traditional guitar-led songs alike.

Ashcroft, McCabe, Jones and Salisbury eventually gravitated towards one another and committed to pool together their dole money and rent rehearsal space at a nearby studio, Splash. For up to eleven hours per session, the quartet would work each other out through improvisation, musically harmonising to create grooves of their own without verbally suggesting ideas. Salisbury cites Ashcroft as the driving force for the band's successes at that early stage, with the singer declaring as much to Jones' father, being met with expected derision. Salisbury, in particular, was focusing more on the band than his degree (in ceramics) at college.

Unusually for any new band from 1955 to this day, no cover versions of songs were ever considered in rehearsal. Despite this, the four friends would use the rest of their time together to absorb musical styles through listening to what Ashcroft refers to as 'the basics' of The Byrds and Buffalo Springfield before moving on to older funk, soul and jazz. In a piece in *Melody Maker* two years later, Ashcroft supplied a list of his favourite records which included The Beach Boys, Sly and the Family Stone, The Stooges and Love. As people bond over music their ears tend to bleed into one another, so it can be assumed that Ashcroft spoke for the band to a certain degree in the 1992 article.

To celebrate the 18th birthday of a friend and flatmate of Ashcroft's, he and his three musical companions (still nameless as a collective entity) performed their first gig at the Honeysuckle Inn pub just outside Wigan, in nearby Poolstock, on 15 August 1990. The setlist consisted of only two songs: The Sun, The Sea and Your Back (sic). One can only surmise the reception they received in their immediate response, which was to not perform for another six months. Under coercion from the frontman, they secured a gig at Manchester's Boardwalk in February 1991, having continued to rehearse regardless of whether they had gigs lined up or not.

An immediate problem quickly presented itself. To feature on listings and simply to generate excitement for the show, a name would have to be given which did justice to the sonic ploughs they were furrowing. Opining that the word meant 'excitement and emotion', they settled on the title 'Verve'.

Local paper *The Wigan Reporter* was effervescent in their praise of the band's set:

> *By the second number they were really cooking on gas, singer Richard had the crowd of over 200 eating out of the palm of his hand. By the end of the eight-song set, the venue had witnessed a truly remarkable debut from a great prospect for 1991.*

Sadly, posterity has thus far not been kind to the setlist, with details of what was included difficult to track down. It can be reasonably surmised that The Sun, The Sea and possibly All in The Mind were played. Regardless, surely emboldened by the positive response, Verve hunkered down and continued to harness their sound throughout the year, with a second night at the Boardwalk just under three weeks later. Throughout March and April 1991, the band kept to their surrounding areas, with gigs in St Helen's, Bolton, Manchester and Wigan before taking in a gig at St Catherine's College in Liverpool in May, with the gigs arranged by their new manager Dave Halliwell. All the while Verve's four members were claiming income from the Department of Health and Social Security (the payment otherwise known as 'The Giro').

The DHSS was a government department responsible for providing a means-tested payment to people on low incomes, such as pensioners or the unemployed, rolled out from 1968. It has undergone several rebrands and adjustments, but British governments of the 21st century have long abandoned the allowance for those out of work to simply sustain their existence. Various programmes under Labour and Conservative administrations have come and gone, with further restrictions set ensuring that the claimant effectively must, or be proactively seeking, work under the Jobseeker's Allowance. In the late 1980s and 1990s, the giro was an invaluable resource to those who were unable to seek work, especially in industrial towns (such as Wigan) which had been victims of Thatcherism.

Eventually being able to scrape together £200 from DHSS money to record a demo tape, Verve rented a portable eight-track studio and used Jones' parents' front room as a venue to record some tracks, which they had also been using as a rehearsal space when the opportunity arose. Never officially released, but available as a bootleg in certain recesses of the internet, *The Wigan Demos* are a fascinating glimpse into how far the band had come, and how far they still had to go.

In the first sessions, the band were able to put down The Sun, The Sea, Verve are Rising along with future singles All in the Mind and Slide Away. Arguably more song-based than what would become their first album, as good as tracks like Here She Comes are, the ethereal nature of Slide Away immediately set a standard to aspire to. Much of Ashcroft was inaudible, but that only added to the effectiveness of portraying him as a mythical and enigmatic frontman in the mould of Jim Morrison.

As was and still is common practice, the group sent their demo tape to WEA, who had shown some interest, as well as other labels A&M, London Records and Island, but all to no avail. However, the tape managed to find its way to Miles Leonard, a man in his first year as a talent scout (A&R) at Hut Records, an affiliate of Virgin Records. Largely credited as relaunching Kylie Minogue's career at the turn of the millennium, Verve were Leonard's first major signing. He would go to become Chairman of Parlophone Records, maintaining this position during Warner Records' acquisition of the label in 2013.

After arranging a gig in London at the Fulham Greyhound, positioned as a showcase for Virgin's hierarchy, Dave Boyd of Hut Records chose to sign the band after what was only their twelfth gig. Boyd, formerly of Rough Trade Records, ran Hut Records as an independent label when it was a subsidiary of Virgin. As a means of gaining exposure for newer artists, Hut was actually younger than Verve as an entity but seemed a perfect fit for the band. The label focused primarily on the UK Indie Chart to gain recognition among their peers and contemporaries. Around the same time, Hut licenced alt-rockers Smashing Pumpkins from Caroline Records in the U.S., Boyd having convinced the American label that his burgeoning outfit was better placed to promote the band's debut album *Gish* than the label's UK arm.

With an approach to signing young artists and allowing them to develop at their own pace, Hut was a perfect fit for the fledgling band of sonic explorers and, once signed in September 1991, the band were left to their own devices for six months, giving them time to develop. Richard Ashcroft would later go on to reveal that the band, surely entirely coincidentally with an advance burning a hole in their pocket, would have the 'most ridiculously indulgent, decadent six months' (i), the singer even going so far as to have his dinner delivered to his home address every night. The money, apparently, soon disappeared. But the gigs continued.

Despite still living in Wigan, the band played the music industry game and made numerous forays to London, still the best option for exposure, to ever-improving reviews. At a gig at the Falcon in Camden, Roger Morton of the *NME* was effervescent in his praise: 'Verve are gigantic… they're an accident in a chemical factory. They are the blinding flash merchants of architectural guitaring. The mysteries of existence in a loop and shimmering chord. An epileptic bastard.' (ii) Morton would go on to praise the young Ashcroft as 'the offspring of Julian Cope and Patti Smith.' Praise in the press continued, with *Melody Maker* listing them as a 'Band for '92', dubbing Ashcroft the 'the sexiest brunette narcissist since Jagger '65'.

The reviews were positive, and the audiences were increasing in size and support, so Verve were in a good place when they entered the Blue Bell Hill studios in Kent in November 1991 to record their debut single: All in the Mind.

Single 1:

All in the Mind
Released: 9th March 1992; UK Chart Position: N/A; Label: Hut Records; Album: N/A

B-sides: One Way to Go; Man Call Sun
Producer: Paul Schroeder
Engineer: Steve Elswood

Unfortunately, the recording sessions were not quite what the band had hoped for, owing to a combination of inexperience on the band's part when it came to the mechanics of recording (rather than playing live) and some serious self-indulgence. As bewitches many a drug taker, the band were convinced that the track would sound equally as good when recorded on LSD as it would when listening back. As many have discovered before and since, this was not the case, but producer Paul Schroeder was eventually able to put together a piece of music that came close to reflecting the aspirations of the band. Unfortunately, despite being one of their stand-out tracks in their burgeoning canon, the process of recording All in the Mind left a scar, and the band rarely, if ever, performed the track live again.

This is a great shame as the song is a screeching, rattling wail of psychedelic sonic artistry with a bone-chilling guitar line from McCabe on the chorus. As a mission statement ('I was born to fly, pretty high') it works well, encouraging the listener to look within ('it's all inside') and prepare themselves for what is to come. As it crosses the three-minute mark, after a hushed breakdown it ups the ante for one final glimpse into the void before suddenly stopping, leaving the listener with a taste in the throat and a thirst for more. The 'learning to fly' elements of the lyrics would add meat to the bones of a nickname that the media were started to apply to the unpredictable frontman: Mad Richard.

The B-sides serve well in showcasing different sides of the band; One Way to Go is a soothing balm after what has come before, no doubt the result of one of the band's lengthy jams. It takes them seven minutes to express themselves when three would do, but it is all the better for it, with a simple but melodic gem of a chorus. Better still is the glistening Man Called Sun (confusingly, an 'A' was added for later versions), a favourite of both band and audience that summons up impossible memories of incense sticks in darkened rooms. With his dub bassline, Simon Jones holds things together while his colleagues explore their respective musical universes.

Yet for all its virtues, Verve's maiden single failed to chart in March 1992. Even though such purveyors of timeless, ambitious music would always sound out of place even among their peers, the UK charts were their usual schizophrenic and varied selves. From the world of alternative music, Nirvana were riding the highs of their *Nevermind* campaign with a strong second single in Come As You Are, while the other side of American rock was lagging behind in the form of Guns N' Roses' November Rain. Closer to home, a band that were surely an influence on Verve (The Jesus And Mary Chain) was also doing well. The inclusion also of Red Hot Chili Peppers' modern classic Under The Bridge elsewhere in the charts suggests US rock was making more of an impact in the UK, with Britpop only in its embryonic stage and the bright stars of shoegaze flickering out.

Indeed, Verve can, with the benefit of hindsight, be viewed as a bridge in British guitar music between Shoegaze and Britpop. The Scene That Celebrates Itself, as dubbed by cynics of the genre, notably *Melody Maker*'s Steve Sutherland, was characterized by distorted, ethereal, visceral soundscapes and loud delayed or reverbed guitars used to create pieces of music more akin to film soundtracks. It is a fair comparison in the case of Verve, with the influences of Cocteau Twins and My Bloody Valentine apparent, as well as the Glaswegians The Jesus and Mary Chain and more recent acolytes to the cause such as Ride and Slowdive. Verve's early work certainly sits well amongst this particular field. In celebration of the single, and as a valuable part of the promotion, Verve adorned the cover of *Melody Maker* for the first time.

The accompanying video for All in the Mind reflected the budget of the first video. Ashcroft was placed at front and centre, initially looking androgynous in black t-shirt and trousers (along with a very fetching John Motson/Del Boy sheepskin jacket) as the band were filmed individually against a white background at director Miles Aldridge's flat. Those shots are cut with others of a car journey through a city or town before Ashcroft is revealed to be dressed as a woman of the night. The sleeve, meanwhile, was the first of many working in conjunction with Brian Cannon.

Cannon had met the young Ashcroft at a party of a mutual friend in Wigan some years earlier and the pair had struck up a conversation over similar interests. Cannon brought it up in conversation that he aspired to be a sleeve designer for bands, which inevitably would have led Ashcroft to mention his outfit. Thinking no more of it, both men went about their respective chosen careers until a chance meeting at a petrol station, whereby the young singer reminded Cannon of their conversation and put him in touch with their manager, David Halliwell. Cannon would go onto design all the band's artwork in the 1990s and would also work with Oasis in the same capacity, as well as Irish three-piece Ash and, more recently, Mancunian three-piece Deja Vega.

Meanwhile, the band were still required to flog their wares around the country and supported both Oxford shoegazers Ride, then space rockers Spiritualized, themselves in their first flush of musical success following debut album *Lazer Guided Melodies*. Following his exit from Spacemen 3, Jason Pierce's singular vision has long been the driving force for a band that has undergone a multitude of different line-ups. At this early point in their burgeoning career, the band was made up of Pierce on vocals and guitars, Mark Refoy on guitars, Will Carruthers (also formerly of Spacemen 3), Jonny Mattock on drums and Kate Radley (at the time Pierce's girlfriend) on keys. This tour was the first time Richard Ashcroft met the woman who would later become his wife.

Both tours were surely influential on Verve's sound, with Pierce wryly commenting later, 'We just went on tour together and they sounded different at the end of it.' (iii) On one of the support slots, at the UEA in Norwich, Verve were disappointed to be playing to an audience of only 15-20 and so performed only two songs (probably still a good ten minutes) before walking offstage. The band would later justify their actions by asking the question, 'What's the point of cheating these people by pretending that Verve are the type of band who just go through the motions?' (iv)

For the release of their second single, and possibly chastened by the experience of recording their first, Verve worked with a new producer (Barry Clempson) and decamped to a new studio (The Manor Studio in Oxfordshire) to attempt to capture their live sound more accurately. At least, that was presumably the initial intention. Clempson, at this point best known for his work with tour-mates Spiritualized, was presumed to be responsible for the slowed-down version of She's a Superstar that saw a commercial release. In a live setting, the track was shorter and faster, whereas the recorded version, with its drawn-out instrumentation, bore little resemblance, but the decision to refresh the track was taken by the band rather than the producer. Verve were in no mood to meet the expectations of a press more used to acts evolving to become more chart-friendly and instead were confident enough to believe that their fans would want to express themselves and hear more from them, rather than less.

Single 2:

She's a Superstar
Released 22 June 1992; UK Chart Position: 66; Label: Hut; Album: *The Verve EP*
B-side: Feel
Producer: Barry Clempson
Mixers: Barry Clempson, Tony Harris

Wonderfully gargantuan but with a minimalist, sparkling chorus, She's a Superstar is early Verve at their grandiose, magnetic best, but perhaps is not for the faint-hearted. B-Side Feel is even more sprawling, clocking in at over ten minutes, and comes and goes like a ghost within its lengthy runtime, tickling and teasing the listener into thinking it may explode into life but never actually doing so. Combined with the near-nine-minute A-side, there was no room for any additional tracks on any of the formats on which the single was released. It did fare better than its predecessor, making a dent in the top 100 of the UK Singles Chart, with a sleeve cover taken in Glossop, Derbyshire. The image would go on to form the basis of the artwork for their Greatest Hits album some years later. She's a Superstar failed to make a dent on the UK Singles chart, coming in at number 66.

Melody Maker gave Verve's latest offering the single of the week once again, and in an accompanying interview with David Stubbs, Richard Ashcroft poured fuel on the fire of his steadily increasing legend as a shamanic frontman: 'When we play live, I've got a million thoughts swimming through my head. And sometimes people mention Damon from Blur as a comparison and that really pisses me off. It trivialises my feelings. Because when we play live, I feel like I'm flying. I'm obsessed with flying. And when we play live, it's the nearest thing to being lifted off this earth.' (v)

Going into more detail about his stepfather's Rosicrucian leanings, he elaborated that 'most of my dreams are about flying, about going away places. I believe in a few years I'll be able to fly. I honestly believe that. Through meditation. I've got a stepfather who's seriously into meditation and I've heard of him raising the temperature in a room or turning sticks in water just through the forces of his mind. Things like that influence me so much. I was stuck in Wigan with no job, but my mind was hundreds of miles away in the sky and in the sea. It's all escapism, about being somewhere else.' (vi)

In the same wide-ranging interview, Ashcroft also claimed that Verve would fold if they ever had to deal with record company interference: 'As long as I'm satisfied, we'll progress, do better gigs, make better records', a statement which, given later events, is a fascinating insight into his mindset. Note the use of 'I' rather than 'we.' Meanwhile, demonstrating that it wasn't just Ashcroft with a singular vision, Nick McCabe offered his view of the band's progressive inclinations: 'This band is totally selfish, self-centred and self-indulgent, and that's exactly the way it should be.' (vii)

Touring once again (but this time as headliners) Verve were now performing at small to mid-range venues, including Windsor's Old Trout and the legendary Joiners' Arms in Southampton. They also performed at the Clapham Grand in south London which, due to no doubt being recorded for posterity, is now regarded as one of their legendary early live shows. This being pre-internet, that is quite easy to quantify as two of the tracks were recorded and included as later B-sides on their next single.

The parent track of which was Gravity Grave, the unruly, wild, black sheep brother of their early canon. Once again held together by simple but solid basslines from Simon Jones, while Pete Salisbury keeps things rumbling on with some subtle, tribal drumming, it's an eight-minute, acid-flecked journey through psychedelia itself. Even the harmonica and flutes sound discombobulated. The snarling but soothing Endless Life completed the set.

Single 3:

Gravity Grave
Released: 5 October 1992; UK Chart Position: 78;
Label: Hut; Album: *The Verve EP*
B-sides: Endless Life; A Man Called Sun (Live at Clapham Grand, 17/07/92); Gravity Grave (Live encore Clapham Grand, 17/07/1992)
Producer: Barry Clempson
Mixers: Barry Clempson, Tony Harris

The tracks were recorded at not one but two new studios (Jacobs Studio in Farnham, with Endless Life being recorded at a studio in Ancoats, Manchester) suggesting their nomadic nature didn't lend itself to consistency of approach while the video, featuring the band driving a 1973 Dodge Charger around a dystopian desert, was amusingly filmed around Hartlepool. The single itself once again failed to break the top 40, coming in at a lower position than its predecessor at number 78.

The band hit the road once again to promote Gravity Grave, playing venues with capacities of a few hundred. One of the shows, at Camden Town Hall in London, was filmed and released as a live video and later re-released as a DVD extra on the *A Storm in Heaven* boxset. The stage divers may date it but it's an excellent watch and, as one of the few existing pieces of footage from the era, gives an insight into what an experience it was to see the band pre-album release. All the ingredients that have become part of the legend are in place: Ashcroft is a confrontational, almost religious frontman that is sometimes channelling Jim Morrison and sometimes channelling Robert Plant. He's also incredibly tactile, either touching the stage, the mic stand, or his own body but always letting the hands do his talking for him.

Pete Salisbury, under-rated as a drummer, is monstrous throughout, particularly on She's a Superstar and the maelstrom of The Sun, The Sea, and his skin skills would become a more powerful weapon in the band's arsenal as time wore on, but the foundations are in place. Nick McCabe operates, as he always did, in his own orbit, seemingly unbothered by crowd or band but every lick, subtle or otherwise, is exactly right. With a band so immersive and with the singer side-lined for long periods at a time, a compelling frontman who can carry the visual load is required (along with an excellently judged fog machine) and Ashcroft carries the responsibility with aplomb, looking at points astonished, righteous or inconsolable.

A few days after the Camden Town Hall gig, the band flew over to New York to take part in the CMJ music marathon. Surely (and somewhat ironically) riffing on a publicity stunt by The Rolling Stones, who performed on the back of a truck down 5th Avenue as part of the promotion for their 1975 US tour, Verve performed for two hours on a truck while driving through the streets of New York. Video footage, available on the *A Storm in Heaven* box set, shows people from all walks of life (as can only be found in the Big Apple) engaging with the set. Given that their setlist was continually expanding, it was a strange choice to fill the two hours with one song: A Man Called Sun was first performed as a 45-minute track and then a half-hour one. Heading back home, Verve supported US rockers the Black Crowes at Brixton Academy, with Ashcroft seemingly taken by the idea of performing barefoot on stage in the same vein as Chris Robinson, singer of the headline act.

December 1992 saw the release of a short compilation album aimed directly for the US market, which the band had seemingly taken to during their visits, and audiences had responded in kind. It's not difficult to see why; with nothing quintessentially British about the band, and with many of their influences deriving from the United States (such as Funkadelic, the Stooges and David Crosby), the possibilities of a cult following were strong. No new material was included, but *The Verve EP* served as a good crash-course of the band's career to date.

EP 1:

The Verve EP
Released 7 December 1992; U.K. Chart Position: N/A;
Label: Vernon Yard (US), Hut Records (UK)
Track Listing: Gravity Grave (edit); A Man Called Sun*; She's a Superstar (edit); Endless Life; Feel
Producers: Barry Clempson, *Paul Schroeder

In a considerate gesture to their UK fans, who were likely to pay exorbitant import prices to get their hands on a copy, Verve made sure that 3000 copies of the vinyl were held back for their home market. Although released on Vernon Yard (another subsidiary of Virgin), it was distributed by Caroline Records in the US. Rounding a successful first year in the public eye off, Verve came fifth in *Melody Maker*'s 'Brightest Hope' poll at the end of the year, as well as winning 8th best single of the year for All in the Mind.

CHAPTER TWO
'You Can Do Anything You Want to, All You've Got to Do is Try' (1992-93)

Plans were afoot for 1993, the most important of which was an album. Nobly, the band did not want to rip their fans off by giving them an album with a track list they had already heard, and so despite having only two songs left in their arsenal (The Sun, The Sea and Slide Away), the band entered Sawmill Studios in Cornwall in a confident mood. Infamously, Sawmills Studios could only be accessed by boat and at specific times, as dictated by the tide.

For a group of musical experimentalists like Verve, the atmosphere and environment would have been conducive to their psychedelic meanderings. The Stone Roses had used Sawmills for their landmark single Fools Gold and the studio would later be used by Oasis for the recording of *Definitely Maybe,* Muse's first two EPs, and other work by Ride, Catatonia and Supergrass, to name a few. John Leckie was chosen to produce.

Leckie already had a formidable track record. As well as producing several singles by The Stone Roses, he was also behind the desk for their seminal self-titled debut, as well as working closely with XTC's Andy Partridge regularly throughout the years. Not only that, but Leckie had also worked on albums by George Harrison (*All Things Must Pass*), John Lennon and Yoko Ono (*Plastic Ono Band*), Paul McCartney (*McCartney*), Pink Floyd (*Wish You Were Here*) and The Fall (*This Nation's Saving Grace*), in various capacities and would later go on to produce Radiohead (*The Bends*) and Muse's second album (*Origin of Symmetry*). By any measurement, it was an impressive CV that made him an ideal candidate for the Wigan four-piece.

As well as being inspired by their surroundings and a healthy supply of marijuana, Leckie was said to expand the band's musical horizons to formulate new ideas and new songs, which were in short supply. Leckie understood that Verve needed to express themselves and allowed them to follow any instinct they felt appropriate, with Richard Ashcroft adding lyrics to the songs as they rambled and progressed, often for significant amounts of time. In the booklet accompanying the *A Storm in Heaven* deluxe edition, Pete states 'I was into the drums on Dr. John's *Gris-Gris* album and Michael Shrieve's playing on David Crosby's *If I Could Only Remember My Name.'* (viii)

Elsewhere, the band were big fans of *Fun House* by the Stooges and were influenced enough by the twisted brass sections that they put their own take on The Sun, The Sea. Although Nick McCabe had a pregnant girlfriend back in Wigan and therefore felt unable to engage fully, it's not apparent on the record, with his guitar parts equally thrilling and unsettling. Having seen UK label-mates The Smashing Pumpkins at the Underworld in Camden, Verve had become fans of their debut album *Gish* and pilfered the 'loud/quiet' technique for Already There, while the remainder of the tracks were said to find life organically, the four members of the band rehearsing or recording when facing each other in a bid to translate the intensity of their live performances.

Star Sail introduces the band with a crashing guitar before setting down and building back up again, Ashcroft accompanied by what sounds like a choir of Tibetan monks. As on much of the album, the singer's voice is gentler and more delicate than his trademark baritone which would come later. Wispier, it suits the ethereal nature of the music. Already There is *barely* there at first but seeps into the listener's consciousness. Like a punch in the leg, it dulls the senses powerfully with a seductive but anxious simple strum of the guitar. Even more fragile is Beautiful Mind, as the album slows to a glacial but tranquil pace in the mid-section which makes it more compelling,

McCabe's shimmering guitar capturing the imagination in particular.

The Sun, The Sea is the angry, snarling Uncle of the early demo complete with rambunctious brass, which betrays Richard Ashcroft's inexperience as a chorus writer (which would improve over time) and is consequently an interesting listen, although the defiance that would be a staple of his interviews is present and correct. ''Cos when the feelings there shattered and scared/I know, you've won, goodbye, I'm gone,' he cries, perhaps referring to an unrequited relationship. Virtual World has a western swagger, with pleasant flutes contributing to a feeling of walking laconically through the countryside on a sunny day. Make it 'til Monday is a conversation as an out-of-body experience, Ashcroft's vocals even lower in the mix and drenched in effects.

Butterfly is the gunslinger of the pack, gospel-laden but with the devil in its stride, swampy but snapping like a drunken alligator. It almost goads the listener into defying it across its near-seven minutes of pagan ritual as music with the band at full throttle. In contrast, the closing track See You in The Next One (Have A Good Time), an Ashcroft only composition but credited to the band, is hymnal, the brushed guitar and solitary tambourine conveying the desolate, melancholy nature of the lyrics. A wonderful closer and a sign of things to come.

Otherwise, the lyrical content is shrouded in mystery or, more specifically, ambiguity. Every inch playing up to the hippie stereotypes, even the lyrics are more about feeling than listening. God, or an equivalent, is often represented as 'she', although Ashcroft did have a long-term girlfriend at the time and, given how his later songs would always eulogise about love, the 'she' in question may be that person.

As a benchmark for how far the band had come in a short space of time *A Storm in Heaven* is remarkable, as Nick McCabe himself noted, "The band that Virgin signed, we ditched early on. The early demos were like Rolling Stones power-pop tunes. They bore no relation to what ended up on *A Storm in Heaven*. We'd moved on already.' (cviv) Also recorded during the sessions were two tracks, one of which saw the light of day 23 years later, on the reissue: Shoeshine Girl and South Pacific. Both tracks are interesting but inessential. A session version of another track (Brake Lights) was also included on the reissue.

With a title that took its name from a book about the effects LSD had on American culture, and with a fitting cover image by Brian Cannon (each image on the artwork representing a stage of life: birth, youth, middle-age and old age. For example, the burning car represents the folly and recklessness of the adolescent years for a human), the album was completed in early 1993 and earmarked for a summer release. Before that, Verve treated their American audience to another exclusive: a live EP, or a 'limited-edition official bootleg'. Once again conscious of their home fans, Verve insisted that some of the 1000 copies of the record, consisting of live recordings at gigs in New York and London, would be available in the UK. Upping the limited-edition element even further, 300 copies were damaged in transit, and the album is now available for a cool $1000.

EP 2:

Voyager 1
Released: March 1993; UK Chart Position: N/A; Label: Jolly Roger
Track Listing: Slide Away; Gravity Grave; One Way to Go; South Pacific; Already There; She's a Superstar

Voyager 1 (we are still waiting for volume two) kept things ticking over and placated the fans who had been waiting patiently for six months for new Verve music. They didn't have to wait long, with the first single lifted from *A Storm in Heaven* released in May 1993.

Single 4:

Blue
Released: 10 May 1993; U.K. Chart Position: 69; Label: Hut Records; Album: *A Storm in Heaven*
B-Sides: Twilight**; Where the Geese Go*; No Come Down*
Producers: John Leckie; *Verve: **Barry Clempson

Meanwhile, for the US market, after undergoing a remix, 'Blue' was released with a sparkling new video and alternative B-sides:

Blue (US version)
Label: Vernon Yard Records
Track Listing: Blue (USA Mix); 6 O'clock; Make it 'till Monday (acoustic); Virtual World (acoustic)
Producers: John Leckie
Producer, mixer: Barry Clempson

To this listener's ears, there is negligible difference between the two mixes, the driving, marauding nature of the song not losing any power as it went over the pond. More differences can be found in the two videos; the US version is a relatively straight-forward video of the band performing (largely lifted from their Camden Town Hall gig), whereas the UK version picks up where the Gravity Grave video left off with a more agitated, stuttering filming style which reflects the tempo of the song while the band visits an underground den, akin to the club in Quentin Tarantino's *From Dusk 'til Dawn*.

Blue was the only new song from the Sawmills sessions that was anywhere near approaching radio-friendly, as Leckie attested in the *A Storm in Heaven* box set notes: 'The only real single we turned up was Blue, which was the song that we made up in the studio it came from one of those backwards experiments I used to do with The Stone Roses. We played the tape backwards and created another song from it.' (ix)

According to Simon Jones, Richard Ashcroft was still finishing his vocals at 6am on the morning Dave Boyd, MD of Hut, was collecting the master recordings for the album. It's interesting to note the progress of the band at this point; having already moved on from their early work when entering the studio, the whole process empowered the group with a bit more nous as to what would be acceptable to the masses, and therefore where they would go next if they wanted to continue their trajectory. Ashcroft certainly sounds more assertive on Blue than on previous singles.

Of the tracks on the UK release, Twilight twinkles like a sunrise with laconic harmonica, Where the Geese Go aims for beauty, with some impressively high-pitched wailing from Ashcroft, but ultimately comes up a bit short and errs on the side of inconsequential and No Come Down, barring one verse an instrumental, is a shuffling acoustic number which is mainly mood music. The US release has less to offer; 6 O'clock attempts to capture the feeling of that time of the morning following the night before, gradually upping the noise levels until the full force of the band is unleashed midway through, then dropping again. As was common practice in the 1990s, two album tracks get the acoustic treatment, presumably in lieu of any new songs. Both Make it 'till Monday and Virtual World are complemented by their acoustic versions but, aside from more assertive lead vocals, don't offer much else for anyone other than the hardcore fans.

Verve's near eight-month absence from the UK Top 100 saw the band return to a familiar scenario of a characterless singles chart and, even disregarding their unique sound, Verve were standing alone but still struggling to make any significant impact, scraping into the Top 70 at number 69.

Promotion for *A Storm in Heaven* began in late Spring, with Richard Ashcroft giving more insight into his beliefs (or lack of) which resulted from his father's death in an interview with Andrew Smith of *Melody Maker*: 'I remember being picked up by a friend, a vicar's son. He took me to his house, and I remember thinking, 'right, religion's out from this day on,' and having a serious argument with him in the car. That was important for me because it hardened me, made me feel less respectful of life. I know how easy it is to be wiped out in a day, how possible it is to disappear in a second. I gained an awareness of how quickly people can leave you and of how little time you've got to enjoy yourself, and show yourself off, and have relationships with people. If he (his father) was alive I wouldn't be here with Verve right now. I'd swap it to have him back, but I guess you can't do that.' (x)

Elsewhere in the same interview, Ashcroft took those who had gleefully dubbed him 'Mad Richard' to task, as he was (and is) always prone to. At the same time defending himself and outlining his passion, the singer said, 'The thing is, Nick and the others are cutting the music and I'm just interpreting it. I'm probably 15/16 different people during a gig you, know? Sometimes I just disappear, and I wouldn't swap it for the world, that feeling of being totally elevated, totally blown away. World War Three could be taking place around the corner, but I wouldn't hear it or see it because of those few moments of complete abandon. That's the greatest thing in the world. A lot of people think music is three chords and strange haircuts when it's so much more than that.' (xi)

He also went into detail about the state of rock music as a whole: 'I think people who saw us last year thought we were a bit hyped, or something to do with Suede. They were completely wrong. There's always a tendency for people to exaggerate your place in the world. I mean, to the vast majority of people, Verve, Suede, Spiritualized, even U2, mean nothing at all. But to me, this is everything. I think about music all the time and I'll never stop believing that we can live up to anything anyone says about us.' (xii)

The name Suede, those southern fops, was cropping up a lot in interviews and the music press in general, the band having been declared British indie's great white hopes with Verve the second name to be suggested when new music was being discussed. Despite sounding nothing alike but both being guitar-based, it demonstrates the real paucity, chart-wise, of British bands of the era, as Manic Street Preachers were suffering from second album syndrome, namely a lot less generosity from the press. All that would soon change as Britpop flickered into life. Having been lumped together with Suede, the not-particularly-British Wiganers would part ways with them (in terms of comparisons) after the release of their debut album.

Album 1:

A Storm in Heaven
Released: 21 June 1993; UK Chart Position: 27; Label: Hut Records
Track Listing: Star Sail; Slide Away; Already There; Beautiful Mind; The Sun, The Sea; Virtual World; Make it 'til Monday; Blue; Butterfly; See You in The Next One (Have A Good Time)
Producer: John Leckie

A Storm in Heaven had a healthy mixture of positive to ecstatic reviews from the mainstream press, with a notably glowing review from *Melody Maker* and three stars from five in *Select*. *Q* magazine's Stuart Maconie, now of BBC *6Music*, posited that 'ultimately, their undoing may be that their fame rests entirely upon journalistic whim, rather than any groundswell of popular support.' (xiii) An interesting thought which seemed entirely possible at the time but was thoroughly disproved, as their success towards the end of the decade put them very much as a band of the people. It hit number 27 in the UK Album Chart.

An added route for exposure was a surprising use of an album track by Hollywood. Ira Levin's novel *Sliver* was the latest attempt to corner the erotic thriller genre by a post-*Basic Instinct* Sharon Stone in a film directed by Phillip Noyce. Critically panned but hitting number 1 at the American box office, the eclectic soundtrack included Star Sail, as well as UB40's cover of Elvis Presley's Can't Help Falling in Love (which sat in the upper reaches of the pop charts) and other luminaries such as Massive Attack, Neneh Cherry and (of course) Shaggy. By anyone's measure, *A Storm in Heaven* had to be considered a success, all the more so given that Nick McCabe, the oldest member of the band, was 21 when they entered Sawmills Studio.

In conjunction with their maiden appearance at Glastonbury Festival, which saw the band earn plaudits (some tracks were recorded for later releases), the album saw the comparisons with Suede dry up as the two bands took very different paths. Suede were regaling audiences with emotional tales of kitchen-sink melodrama, whereas Verve were heading into space.

But their flights were curtailed by the first of several legal wrangles. Presumably unknown to the band, Verve was also the name of a US record label specialising in jazz releases, which was established in the 1940s by

Norman Granz. In conjunction with Deutsche Grammophon (who owned the rights to Verve records), Polygram (who were releasing the jazz label's catalogue) filed a trademark infringement suit in the US District Court of Los Angeles (just as the band were showcasing their new album in the States), on 7 May 1993, intending to seek an injunction against Verve using the name commercially, as well as damages and any profits the band had made.

Not only were the four members of the band listed as defendants, but so too were Virgin Recordings, Hut Recordings and even Caroline Records, distributors of the band's work in the United States. This ongoing case, combined with the prospect of launching Verve in the States, was a catalyst for the decision made by Dave Halliwell to step down as their manager. It was an extremely gracious and honest move; he knew his inexperience may be problematic when it came to breaking new ground for the band, on the cusp of bigger things as they were.

That said, Halliwell's replacements were equally inexperienced in management terms. Phil Savage and John Best had been successful as publicists for Suede (yep, them again) but the duo took the bull by the horns, encouraging Verve to curb some of their more extravagant ideas, such as lengthy singles. The management change did not affect the band's touring as they supported US label mates The Smashing Pumpkins across Europe.

The second and final single selected from soon-to-be-The Verve's debut was released in September 1993 and was an obvious choice, being the only other track on the album that was commercially viable. Thematically, the video for Slide Away bears resemblance to Gravity Grave as the band stride through a desert in Almeria (a clear sign of the money being invested in the band) before heading to a brother to socialise with its workers. The track itself, one of the band's oldest, benefits from experience in a more impassioned delivery by Ashcroft and a climactic structure.

Single 5: Slide Away Released 20 September 1993; UK Chart Position: 90; Label: Hut Records; Album: *A Storm in Heaven* B-Sides: Make it 'til Monday (acoustic); Virtual World (acoustic) Producer: John Leckie

Undoubtedly due to the song already being available on its parent album for a few months, Slide Away scraped into the top 100, peaking at number 90 during the first week of sales. Not that Richard Ashcroft seemed to care about comparisons with any peers. In a now-infamous interview with *Q* magazine's Stuart Maconie, he explained the context in which he saw his band, 'I'm into great music. The music of history. Funkadelic, Can, Sly Stone, Neil Young, the Stones, Chuck Berry, jazz. I hate indie music. It's so diluted and boring, those fast shuffley drums and those guitars. I can name fifty bands who are doing OK now and in two years they will be forgotten. They're just this summer's T-shirt. History will forget them. But history has a place for us. It may take us three albums, but we will be there.' (xiv)

Without question, this has become Richard Ashcroft's most famous quote and for good reason, namely, because it was unerringly accurate as well as ambitious, although perhaps also not a great advert for the yet-to-be-recorded second album. It was fortuitous that he didn't go so far as to name any of the bands he was thinking of, as surely Radiohead and Suede were on his mind at the time, which would have seriously undermined the quote with the benefit of hindsight. The young singer also gave short shrift to the nickname that refused to go away; 'Mad Richard! Pah! If people think that I'm crazy, then it's a sign of the times. It just shows how banal things have become in the last twenty years, how far we've come from the abandon and the entertainment of the past. If I'm Mad Richard, what would they make of Jimi Hendrix? They'd put him in an asylum.' (xv)

After their first headline tour of the United States across October and November, Verve returned home for yet another tour of their home country, with support from LA band Acetone (US label mates who also supported Verve on the American leg) and a fellow North-West act called Oasis.

And so began one of the longest friendships from 1990s rock. With their over-whelming self-belief and attitude towards music (namely being in it for the long haul to stand alongside the greats), Richard Ashcroft found his musical soul mates in Noel and Liam Gallagher. As we'll come to see later, the two acts would weave in and out of each other's career paths frequently from this point on. Verve had been impressed by a demo tape of Oasis that had been doing the rounds in musical circles and offered them the support slot. The tape contained Live Forever, the sort of timeless classic rock track that Ashcroft and his cohorts were continually aiming for, and further emphasised that Verve and Oasis were cut from the same cloth.

The relationship was surely strengthened during the tour (for which the first 100 punters through the door were given a special flexi-disc containing their performance of Make it 'til Monday at Glastonbury, apart from at London's Astoria 2 where the first 200 entrants were bestowed with the gift) and especially at Newcastle's Riverside. Fifteen minutes into their headline set, the PA system cut out and so Verve were left to entertain the crowd via other means. Stepping in to assist, Noel Gallagher joined Ashcroft and McCabe in singing She'll Be

Coming Round the Mountain while Oasis' rhythm guitarist Paul 'Bonehead' Arthurs provided percussion via playing spoons.

Verve had been regulars at the top of the indie charts, as Hut Records met the criteria required (despite their association with Virgin). This changed in December 1993 when Virgin announced that Hut's output would henceforth be distributed by EMI. Fittingly, given their disdain for the classification, Verve were no longer an indie band.

After the relentless touring and steady release of music for the last couple of years, 1994 was a lower-key year for Verve, although not for the lack of trying. Their first headline tour of Europe took place in February, which saw them debut two new songs. Black and Blue, a rambunctious and heavy number that was never recorded, and Mover, which would flit in and out of Verve's consciousness until they finally committed it to record some fourteen years later.

The band were due to perform at Glastonbury Festival once again in the summer but were forced to cancel because Pete Salisbury somehow managed to break his ankle while walking into his kitchen for a glass of water, which also resulted in another show at London's Clapham Grand being cancelled.

Before that, the band's only release of the year was in May to accompany another lengthy American tour and took the form of a compilation album consisting of B-Sides, outtakes and live performances. Entitled *No Come Down* after the B-side, it was once again aimed for the American market but with some copies held back for the British fanbase.

Compilation Album no. 1:

No Come Down
Released: 17 May 1994; UK Chart Position: N/A; Label: Hut Recordings (UK), Vernon Yard (US)
Track Listing: No Come Down, Blue (USA Mix); Make it 'til Monday (acoustic version); Butterfly (acoustic version); Where the Geese Go; 6 O'clock; One Way to Go; Gravity Grave (Live at Glastonbury 1993); Twilight
Producers: The Verve; John Leckie; Paul Schroeder; Nick Green; William Smith; Barry Clempson

No Come Down had the honour of being the first release by the band since the settlement with Verve Records, with a fee of £25,000 being paid to the label in agreement to add a 'The' to their name. Amusingly, before the agreement, the band had offered to rechristen themselves 'Verv' and release the album with the name *Dropping an E for America*, a suggestion which was unsurprisingly not taken up. Because of the name change, sleeve designer Brian Cannon had to superimpose the 'The' onto his already-finished artwork. As a point of clarification to remove any ambiguity, the sleeve notes carried the disclaimer: 'The Verve is not affiliated with the Verve record label, which is a registered trademark of Deutsche Grammophon, licenced to Polygram Records Inc.'

As the freshly minted The Verve continued to tour across the States, they were invited to play at Lollapalooza. Nowadays the festival is a four-day event at one location, but it was originally conceived by Jane's Addiction singer Perry Farrell as a touring circus, and indeed operated like that for the first few years of its inception.

The 1994 edition of the show had a strong alternative line-up, including The Smashing Pumpkins, the

Beastie Boys, George Clinton (formerly of Funkadelic, who The Verve were huge fans of), A Tribe Called Quest, the Breeders and Nick Cave and the Bad Seeds among others performing on its main stage, with the original headliners Nirvana pulling out before Kurt Cobain's suicide earlier in the year. However, the format of the show meant that the performers were required to put on 23 performances as the travelling carnival covered the length and breadth of America. The Verve shared the second stage with The Flaming Lips, Luscious Jackson, Rollerskate Skinny and The Frogs, the actual structure playing very much second fiddle to the main stage, it often being little more than a car park.

At the Sandstone show, The Verve hit troubled waters. Immediately after coming off stage, Richard Ashcroft started convulsing. Paramedics were immediately called but took 25 minutes to reach him because of the vast sprawling site of the festival. The singer was put in an ambulance and dispatched to hospital. Upon his arrival, he was found to be dehydrated by seven litres, which was a consequence of both the 110-degree heat and a marathon drinking session with members of the Bad Seeds and the Breeders.

Ashcroft would later claim that he was so hot that ice was melting off his chest. It was reportedly a life-changing incident for the singer, who was grateful just to be alive, but it didn't prevent him from playing the next day as Lollapalooza rolled into St Paul, Minneapolis. Kim Deal of the Breeders infamously said to their crowd during their performance, 'Did you see Verve? You'd better go see them quick, before they die.' (xvi) It made Ashcroft and company the talk of the tour and added to their legend, although the stresses of the laborious programme forced some cracks to show, with Richard Ashcroft and Nick McCabe apparently barely on speaking terms.

Undeterred, The Verve played several festivals in Europe for the remainder of the summer, including

Reading Festival which was their last live performance of the year. Before the Berkshire gig, The Verve performed at Hultsfred festival in Sweden, alongside their friends Oasis and their Creation label-mates Primal Scream, with the three acts staying at the same hotel.

With the benefit of hindsight and legend, it is a laughable idea that the three acts were even in the same country let alone the same hotel, given their legendary hellraising antics, although The Verve very much came in third in the riotous stakes to both the Gallagher brothers (and Bonehead) and Bobby Gillespie and company. After the festival, the three bands convened at their hotel bar but were served only a handful of rounds before the bar shut. The bands kicked up a fuss, as liquor bottles and furniture were thrown out of the window (in the great tradition of rock and roll), with Ashcroft and Noel Gallagher apparently so desperate for booze that they broke into a local church to drink the communion wine. The police were inevitably called and upon their arrival, with Primal Scream nowhere to be seen, The Verve and Oasis agreed to pay the hotel £800 in damages which the two bands split between them.

CHAPTER THREE
'Finding Myself Used to be Hard, But Now I See the Light' (1995)

At the end of 1994, Richard Ashcroft split with his long-term girlfriend Sarah Carpenter after six years. Sadly, it was not an ordinary breakup as Carpenter had fallen in love with one of The Verve's roadies, Andy Burke, who also happened to be one of Ashcroft's closest friends. Unsurprisingly, the break-up had a deep effect on the singer and, with the specific circumstances exacerbating his grief, he ran away from Wigan firstly to London, and then out to the countryside. The effects of this period would be one of the key themes of The Verve's next album.

And afterwards. In an interview for *Melody Maker* with Dave Simpson during the promotion of *A Northern Soul,* Ashcroft and Simon Jones had a terse exchange of words about the effect that the breakup had had on the band and the recording sessions. A few years after that, before the successful homecoming gig at Haigh Hall, Carpenter sold her side of the story to the *Daily Mirror.*

It wasn't only Ashcroft who had personal troubles before (and during) the recording of their second album. Jones was reportedly trying to assimilate everything that had happened during the previous few years and found himself to have been somewhat drained by the madness while Nick McCabe split up with his pregnant girlfriend around the same period.

Perhaps looking to lose themselves in music, the band reconvened at their old rehearsal space in Wigan to bash out some songs before going into a recording studio (presumably having learned lessons from going into an expensive studio unprepared), sometimes driving around the streets at night waiting for further inspiration. Amidst this, Ashcroft went to London to try and repair his relationship with Carpenter. He was gone for three months and would later admit to excessive hedonism for two of those months.

The band initially attempted to record the LP at said rehearsal room, but this idea was soon scrapped as it became logistically difficult. Instead, they headed to Loco Studios in Wales with two albums' worth of material, having written several songs while touring. As Simon Jones attests in the *A Northern Soul* deluxe edition boxset notes, 'We came off the tour with the album pretty much in the bag. We knew exactly what kind of record we were going to make. We didn't want a repeat of what happened with *A Storm in Heaven*, where we didn't have any material when we were going in to record.' (xvii)

When it came to production duties, The Verve and their management team settled on Owen Morris, apparently, on Noel Gallagher's recommendation. Morris, a larger-than-life Welshman, had recently completed work on *Definitely Maybe*, the debut album by Oasis. Now lauded as one of the best debut albums of all time, the album had undergone an incredibly frustrating gestation with several attempts at translating Oasis' raucous sound to tape found wanting. Brought in by Oasis manager Marcus Russell, Morris cultivated a 'wall of sound' approach to the album, compressing the final mix to an extent that, in simple terms, made the record louder and therefore more reflective of the band.

Given that The Verve had faced similar problems in the past and impressed by the overall bombast of *Definitely Maybe* (and possibly by its commercial success), Morris was an obvious choice to work with them. The Welshman visited The Verve when they were rehearsing in Wigan and was already familiar with the songs selected for their second album.

The sessions for what would become *A Northern Soul* were legendarily debauched. Tales that have emerged include Richard Ashcroft wrecking a hire car by spinning it round and round the studio lawn until the wheels dropped off; The Verve playing just one song (any song) for hours on end; Richard Ashcroft disappearing once again, this time for five days, and the band also considered destroying a tape machine worth £100,000 to simply create a suitably destructive closing sound for the album. Finally, during the recording sessions, the speakers had to be wrapped in chicken wire because they were frequently getting trashed by either band or producer.

However, the first few weeks of the sessions were productive, with Nick McCabe going on to say, 'The first three weeks were the best three weeks of my life because we were just enjoying making music and not thinking about it' (xviii). Inspired by Miles Davis (specifically his album *Bitches Brew*), Funkadelic, Gram Parsons, The Bride Ship's album *Crime + The City Solution* and copious amounts of ecstasy, the sessions were fruitful. The feel-good effects of the drug-taking would have no doubt contributed to the positive atmosphere, but for Nick McCabe, things started to take a dark turn, 'And then it all went nuts. Richard and Owen were shouting and smashing things up and I was retreating into myself. At the end it was horrible.' (xix)

McCabe elaborates in the *A Northern Soul* boxset notes, 'No amount of praise worked for me. I don't like being told everything's alright when it's not. It's OK for things to unravel so long as you've got a plan. I had ridiculous standards of what I wanted, and they were kind of foggy as well.' (xx) While the rest of the band felt the recording was going well, McCabe was starting to have doubts, fuelled by the drug intake and his personal circumstances. As before, Ashcroft's lyrics would be added to whatever soundscapes his three bandmates had concocted, a method that had served The Verve well up to this point.

That was until December 1994, when Richard Ashcroft approached his colleagues to tell them that he had written two songs all by himself. One track was a plaintive ballad called On Your Own and the other was built on an excerpt from William Blake's poem *London*. As Jones explains in the boxset notes, 'He sat down and played History on his acoustic guitar and all our jaws hit the floor. We were like, "Fucking hell! That's an incredible song." We recorded it that night.' (xxi) Jones goes on to speculate that Ashcroft chose to play the song to the bassist, Pete Salisbury and Owen Morris but without Nick McCabe present because the singer would have been too intimidated to play it to 'the musical one'. Upon hearing it, the guitarist felt that he couldn't add anything to the song and so opted not to play on the recording, but Richard Ashcroft took this as a slight.

'I had to take the editorial decision that it was better without me,' McCabe explains on the boxset notes. 'At the time I couldn't summon the spirit and I realised that the writing was on the wall – Richard wanted to work apart from me.' (xxii) In addition to McCabe's state of mind, the incident contributed to the mounting tension within the group, surely exacerbated by Virgin throwing money at the track; a 30-piece string section, along with Will Malone (string arranger for Massive Attack's Unfinished Sympathy) was assigned, with the strings to be recorded at Abbey Road Studios. Ashcroft, Jones, Salisbury and Morris visited the world-famous studios to watch the strings being recorded, and there was a big party atmosphere when it was completed. Brian Cannon and Liam Gallagher were in attendance and added handclaps to the track. McCabe chose not to attend.

The title of the record had a few meanings. Firstly, and most obviously, it was said to be inspired by northern soul, the musical movement which had its spiritual home at Wigan Casino. More personally, Ashcroft was putting words to his recent life experiences as well as Noel Gallagher's, who had quit Oasis while they were touring America in autumn 1994. The Oasis songwriter had disappeared to San Francisco for a few days after a bad show in LA and, continuing the spirit of kinship, Ashcroft felt compelled to write about Gallagher's experiences, with the title being both an acknowledgment and a tribute.

As an aside, in an interview with John Harris of the *NME* in May 1994, Ashcroft would wax lyrical about their Mancunian friends, 'Oasis are honest. They make soul music. It's coming from Noel and the band's hearts. When we toured with them, it was a brilliant feeling, 'cos for so long I felt so isolated, like, 'Where are they? Where are our soul brothers?' And all of a sudden, this band appear from a proper music-loving background. They don't want to be MTV presenters, do they?' (xxiii)

Despite their internal issues, the members of The Verve were unanimous in their praise for their second album. Simon Jones described it as 'soul music', Ashcroft declared himself to be 'elated' and even Nick McCabe called it 'the best album of the last twenty years.' Sadly, the music was not enough to save McCabe spiralling into suspected depression when he returned home from the sessions, with the guitarist believing that the excessive amount of marijuana smoked affected his serotonin levels. This was a problem that would not be going away.

In support of their forthcoming lead single, The Verve were due to support Oasis (the bands swapping places from their previous tour together) for a UK tour (and one date in Paris) and played the first show at The Cliffs Pavilion in Southend. The headline slot was later released on video as *Live by The Sea* but sadly with no sign of Ashcroft and co. The tour then moved on to Paris, but all plans were curtailed, as McCabe was involved in an incident with a bouncer at the famous Bataclan. Unable to produce his pass to get backstage, McCabe was punched in the face and thrown down a flight of stairs, resulting in a broken finger and six weeks in plaster which meant he wouldn't be able to play guitar. As a result, all shows were cancelled.

The injuries didn't affect the release of the first single from the album, which was chosen to be This Is Music, the best representation of The Verve's new sound. The now-familiar bass line (later sampled by Sleaford Mods on the track Urine Mate (Welcome to The Club) from their debut album *Austerity Dogs* in 2013) stings before the rest of the band kicks in urgently and set about to batter the senses. While it still doesn't have a chorus to speak of, there is a brashness not previously present.

The difference between the production styles of John Leckie and Owen Morris is immediately apparent, the latter's style much more confrontational and, simply put, louder. It is also the point where the fully finished Richard Ashcroft emerges, with his now trademark baritone vocal delivery given its first full outing. In the accompanying video, with his cropped hair and sunglasses, he is much more rock star than shaman. The lyrics also covered new ground, with the opening line 'I stand accused, just like you, of being born without a silver spoon' (also prominent on the sleeve) a slight on the upper classes, successfully adding a socio-political element to Ashcroft's palette and arguably, his first lyrics with real resonance. The singer felt that any political observations in music had lost their power and set about redressing the balance. He had recently met someone who had gone to Eton and soon realised that this person had so many more life options available to him than people like Ashcroft and his associates.

The B-sides reflected the two sides of this new Verve. Let the Damage Begin is music as machinery, grinding righteously and, like the A-side, is heavy, intense, and almost industrial. In contrast, You and Me is much more melodic and elegant, with Ashcroft exposing himself through music in the vein of David Crosby.

Single 6:

This is Music
Released: 1 May 1995; UK Chart Position: 35; Label: Hut Records; Album: *A Northern Soul*
B-Sides: Let the Damage Begin; You and Me
Producer: Owen Morris

The various hardships of recording the album and the single, as well as their associations with Oasis and Owen Morris, paid off instantly; the track charted at number 35 in its first week. In their eighteen months away the music scene had changed. Oasis had kicked the doors open for British rock, having hit the number 1 slot the week before with Some Might Say, but also with four of their previous singles in the top 75.

Young upstarts Supergrass, also in the top 10, were representative of the new breed of bands who were gaining critical acclaim and commercial success. Elsewhere in the charts Shed Seven had also broken the top 40, a revitalised Paul Weller (lumped in with Britpop despite his age and experience) was in fashion once again and, interestingly, a track called Born Slippy by Underworld hovered just outside the top 40. Upon its re-release six months later, it would become one of the defining anthems of the era.

It may not have broken into the mainstream consciousness which the same effectiveness as Oasis, Supergrass, etc. but breaking the top 40 for the first time was a measurement of both success and progress for the former space cadets. Two members of the band were also experiencing happiness in their personal lives; Simon Jones had married on Valentine's Day 1995 while Richard Ashcroft had started dating Kate Radley, formerly of Spiritualized. He would go on to marry Radley in the summer of 1995, about a month before her former band began recording their masterpiece *Ladies and Gentlemen We are Floating in Space.*

Strangely, the second single taken from *A Northern Soul* was released just over a month later and was, once again, unlike anything thus far released by The Verve.

Single 7:

On Your Own
Released: 12 June 1995; UK Chart Position: 28; Label: Hut Records; Album: A Northern Soul
B-Sides: I See the Door*; Little Gem; Dance on Your Bones*
Producers: Owen Morris; *The Verve

With no build-up or instrumentation, On Your Own bursts into life from a standing start, Ashcroft's voice, the band, and the winding melody instantly bewitching the listener. Much more straightforward as a song than the meanderings of *A Storm in Heaven* or the bludgeoning of This Is Music, the influence of not only Noel Gallagher but also The Smiths can be felt, the lyric 'you come in on your own and you leave on your own,' is similar to a line from the classic How Soon Is Now? ('and you stand on your own and you leave on your own,'). Either way, as a songwriter Ashcroft was instantly formidable.

Of the B-sides, I See the Door is the pick of the bunch, another acoustic-driven number with an unremarkable verse offset by a subtly heart-breaking bridge and chorus. Little Gem certainly doesn't do what it says on the tin in comparison to the two previous tracks, and Dance on Your Bones feels like a hangover from the previous album, unrestrained in its near-eight-minute runtime. The single release was another progressive step, breaking the top 30 at number 28.

The summer of 1995 is now regarded as one of the high-water marks of Britpop, with the infamous 'Battle of The Bands' between Blur and Oasis taking place in August and the rise of Pulp being the two tentpoles. After years (and years) of obscurity, the Sheffield band headlined Glastonbury Festival after The Stone Roses were forced to pull out and their recent single Common People was an instant anthem, covering similar subject matter to This Is Music but much more commercially viable. However, no matter how powerful a musical movement may be, pop will always win out, as demonstrated by the presence of Robson & Jerome, (TV stars made good, dominating the singles chart for seven weeks with their version of Unchained Melody), Danish pop sensation Whigfield (Think of You) and Wet Wet Wet (Don't Want to Forgive Me Now).

Creatively, The Verve were on the crest of a wave with additional songs not included on *A Northern Soul* in their back pockets. When they were finally able to recommence touring, The Verve debuted a new song (Come On) at a show in Manchester and during an interview with Gareth Grundy of *Select* magazine, Richard Ashcroft referred to a song he had just written: 'There's a new track I've just written. It goes, "the drugs don't work, they just make me worse, and I know I'll see your face again." That's how I'm feeling at the moment. They make me worse, man. But I still take them. Out of boredom and frustration, you turn to something else to escape. Sometimes you've got to go through these things to taste the extremes. I'm attracted to it, in a macabre sort of way. But whenever I pick up a guitar, and right now, I'm automatically tapping into the darker side of my nature. I can't help it, just happens like that.' (xxiv)

In another interview, for *Guitar* magazine, Ashcroft outlined his approach to his and the band's creativity; 'I'm very mixed up in my head between grooves and song writing and I want to get to a beautiful balance.

We want the rhythm section and the guitars to go off on it, but underneath there to be a solid, soulful song. If we can manage that perfectly that'll be the best for me.' In the same interview, Owen Morris offered up his thoughts on the maverick Nick McCabe: 'without a shadow of a doubt the most gifted musician I've ever worked with. I haven't got a clue where his genius comes from. But at the same time, he's a complete and utter nightmare, haha! He'll never play the same song twice. Now you can ask Noel Gallagher to play the same guitar line a hundred times, and as long as there's good reason for him doing it, he'll do it. But with Nick, you've got no chance. But that's what he does, y'know?'. More modestly, in the same interview, McCabe described himself as 'playing the St Helen's blues'. (xxv)

Elsewhere, in an interview with Paul Moody published in *Dazed & Confused,* Ashcroft gave his thoughts on Britpop, with The Verve inevitably being lumped in with the scene, 'We're not part of anything. All these groups at the moment are supposedly punk influenced, well if anybody is influenced by punk, it's us. That is, if punk means doing your own thing and avoiding all the things that you're supposed to be doing. Doing things with soul and depth. I think the really exciting things at the moment are going on in dance music, where kids are making records in their bedrooms and garages. As for us, we'll stay on our own. We don't want to be part of anyone's gang. If people want to join us then yeah, great, but we're not looking up to anyone else.'

Tellingly, he went on to say, 'To create a great thing it just takes one thing: yourself. You've just got to know who you are, and your own mind, and slowly you find out who you are, as time goes by. You just have to open your mind a little bit and gradually you realise that it can be opened more and more. What you have to remember is that you just have to take things for what they are.' (xxvi) Taken in context, the comments broadly seemed like bravado but if one looked hard enough, they could see the cracks that were showing.

Amidst the distraction of another Glastonbury performance (where this time McCabe's amps blew up), *A Northern Soul* was finally unleashed.

Album 2:

A Northern Soul
Released: 20 June 1995; UK Chart Position: 13; Label: Hut Recordings
Track Listing: A New Decade; This is Music; On Your Own; So it Goes; A Northern Soul; Brainstorm Interlude; Drive You Home; History; No Knock on My Door; Life's an Ocean; Stormy Clouds; (Reprise)
Producers: Owen Morris; The Verve

From the opening track (A New Decade) with Owen Morris using the same trick he would later utilise for the second Oasis album *(What's the Story) Morning Glory?* (namely a quiet introduction before substantially increasing the volume), The Verve are in new territory. Simon Jones' bass is the foundation on which Pete Salisbury's drums can clatter, Nick McCabe attacks his guitar and Ashcroft can sing with fire in his belly. The whole track is like the first sun of spring through the window, except the sun is a nuclear fireball.

After the two singles, So it Goes takes a step back in time to the gunslinging swagger of days gone by. It's slightly directionless but with more confident production. Ashcroft's pain at his break-up with Sarah Carpenter is apparent in his vocals and the general bleakness of the lyrics ('I'm just a poor little wifeless fella/another drink and I won't miss her'). The ear-scraping sci-fi of the title track ('I'm gonna die alone in bed') elevates the group to higher planes, with shining church organs adding to the noise whirlwind.

The twisting, metallic shuffle of the largely instrumental Brainstorm Interlude is atmospheric if a bit dull, and may have been better served as a B-side, while (Reprise) (a reprise of what? The whole album distilled, perhaps?) is similarly driven by the sky-scraping proficiency of McCabe's guitars. Elsewhere, the dreamy, dubby Drive You Home allows the rhythm section to take centre-stage, with Jones fostering a lethargic, almost wilfully sluggish bassline that acts independently and Salisbury gently but stoically keeping the beat.

No Knock on My Door is all noise, no melody, and is therefore the most successful example of the album fulfilling Ashcroft's intent that it would be 'about feel'. Life's an Ocean is shuffling funk and would be the song that, when performed live, was the best outlet for the band to improvise. Cited as a Stanley Kubrick-style vision of the future, it builds while allowing itself time to breathe. Stormy Clouds picks up the dystopian baton and runs with it, McCabe's intermittent guitars having the power of a hurricane.

The 2016 boxset reissue of the album included a handful of previously unreleased tracks. Brake Lights, once again attempted and abandoned after the first album, is slower and dreamier but still with a danceable rhythm that could be the foundation of The Music, the Leeds band cut from the same cloth as The Verve who emerged in the early 21st century. King Riff is little more than an alternative version of This is Music while Mover and Muhammad Ali were dusted down for *Forth*. Echo Bass, Come On and a track called Funky Jam (later becoming The Rolling People) found their natural home on albums (and accompanying B-sides) later. It is interesting to hear the tracks in embryonic form; the pronouns are altered ('I am the rolling people') for a start, and it is more fraught, less mighty than it would eventually become. Likewise,

Come On is much lower-key and sparse in comparison to the juggernaut that it would become on *Urban Hymns.*

Reviews were much more varied than for *A Storm in Heaven. Q*, *Select,* and *The Guardian* praised the album but *The Independent* hated it and the *NME* were indifferent. The mix of reactions is unsurprising. *A Northern Soul* is an uncompromising and uncomfortable listen, and certainly out of step with the general positivity pervading British music at the time, and yet because of that it has arguably stood the test of time better than most. The three singles are immediately obvious and are almost out of step with the rest of the album which, taken as a whole, is coherent if claustrophobic. With the benefit of hindsight, it is a clear bridge between the sonic ambition of the first album and the more song-based third album.

The patronage by Oasis (by this point one of the biggest bands in the country), the associations with Britpop and a marked improvement in song writing all combined to help *A Northern Soul* on its way to a number 13 spot in the UK album charts. Finally, The Verve were stepping up a gear. A successful US tour was followed by a slot second on the bill in the King Tut's Tent at T in the Park, where they played an eight-song set spanning the past (The Sun, The Sea), the present (This is Music) and the future (Come On). With domestic bliss for Ashcroft and Jones, a successful album under their belts, acknowledgement from their peers and the power of the live shows undiminished, all seemed rosy in The Verve's garden.

Which was why it came as a great shock when, immediately after leaving the stage at T in the Park, Richard Ashcroft told the band's manager, John Best, that The Verve were splitting up.

To be more accurate, Richard Ashcroft was leaving, despite the story of the band breaking up being presented to the press. Apparently underwhelmed by the reactions to recent tours, as well as the tortuous process of recording the album, Ashcroft felt he could not continue without giving less than 100% commitment. Never one to fake it, the singer was always all or nothing. The warning signs were there during the sessions in Ashcroft's disappearance for five days.

In the aftermath of the split, it became apparent that Ashcroft would continue working with Simon Jones and Pete Salisbury, but not Nick McCabe. The guitarist had his own problems, with his fatherly responsibilities making him feel ostracised from the rest of the group and a part-time member during their tour. Earlier in the summer, when asked about his thoughts on Oasis, soul brothers to the rest of the band, McCabe stood apart: 'I'm not into cliques and I avoid it because most bands are knobs.' (xxvii) It seems this general attitude was causing friction with his bandmates.

McCabe also felt the rest of the band were not understanding of his plight and condition. In an interview with *Vox* magazine two years later, McCabe explained, 'I was being a miserable bastard, totally paranoid… so they sacked me. Well, no one was asked to leave but that's how it felt at the time. Me and Richard don't always get on, we're polar opposites.' (xxviii)

Single 8:

History
Released: 18 September 1995; UK Chart Position: 28;
Label: Hut Recordings; Album: A Northern Soul
Track Listing: CD1: History (radio edit); Back on My Feet Again*; On Your Own (acoustic); Monkey Magic (Brainstorm Mix)
CD2: History (Album version); Grey Skies*; Life's Not A Rehearsal
Producers: Owen Morris; *The Verve

The Verve split up in August/September 1995, shortly before the release of the third single to be lifted from *A Northern Soul*, History. As the band were no more, the video for the track was an amalgamation of previous efforts and of course, irony of ironies, it was their biggest hit to date, charting at number 28.

For the first time, The Verve released the singles as two CDs with alternative B-sides, a strategy that surely helped sales. Rarely would the third single from an album, especially one already released, perform better than the previous two releases. Back on My Feet Again, surely also about Ashcroft's relationship with Carpenter, sweeps, soars, and eventually growls and while Grey Skies is slow, what it lacks in urgency it makes up for in ethereal sweep.

Also for the first time The Verve ventured into remix territory, Life's Not A Rehearsal being an alternative version of Life's an Ocean, while the wired psychedelia of Monkey Magic is a Nick McCabe remix. The acoustic version of On Your Own puts as much emphasis on the piano as it does the acoustic guitar, adding yet more heartache to a plaintive song, while Ashcroft's decision not to repeat the falsetto outro and to instead sing in a lower key adds more gravitas.

The sleeve design for the singles featured a band shot underneath a cinema or theatre sign, bearing two different messages, one per sleeve: Life Is Not A Rehearsal and All Farewells Should Be Sudden. The serendipity was not lost on anyone, nor was the irony of the success of History, Ashcroft claiming that he choked up when hearing the song on Radio One. Had they continued to tour *A Northern Soul* for the remainder of 1995 they could have capitalised on its success but Richard Ashcroft, buoyed by his previously unknown song writing ability, had other ideas.

CHAPTER FOUR
'Sometimes in Life You Feel Yourself Rearranging. That's Just the Way it Goes' (1996-97)

In October 1995 Oasis released their second album *(What's the Story) Morning Glory?* which was an immediate commercial success and sent the Mancunians into the stratosphere. At the time of writing, over twenty-five years on, it is the UK's fifth best-selling album and the third best-selling studio album of all time, beaten only The Beatles' *Sgt. Pepper's Lonely Hearts Club Band* and Adele's *21,* ('Best Of' albums by Queen and ABBA taking the top two slots). (xxix) One of the tracks on the album, Cast No Shadow, was 'dedicated to the genius of Richard Ashcroft', an acknowledgement in response to Ashcroft's tip of the hat to Noel Gallagher on *A Northern Soul.* This gesture added fuel to the mythology and legend of The Verve, who were already becoming known to the wider public via History and the split.

Hut Recordings were keen to continue working with Ashcroft who, as well as proving his success as a songwriter with On Your Own and History, was outspoken and photogenic and therefore would be an easy sell to the rock star-hungry public. It seems that Ashcroft also had plans, regularly visiting managers John Best and Phil Savage with ideas of who he was going to work with. Eventually, he decided that he would continue working with Simon Jones and Pete Salisbury and still disenchanted with Nick McCabe, set about finding a guitarist. He eventually contacted an old friend from Winstanley, Simon Tong. Tong was a capable musician, able to contribute both guitar and keyboards, and given his background and friendship with the band's members, slotted into the existing dynamic with little trouble. He was, after all, the person who had taught Jones and Ashcroft how to play the guitar all those years ago.

While Salisbury, Jones and Tong moved to London to await instructions, Ashcroft and his new wife Radley moved to Bath, where the singer threw himself into music. He set about teaching himself the basics of music such as tempo, rhythm, and dynamics, before a creative spurt led to the compositions and demo recordings of Space and Time, Sonnet, Bitter Sweet Symphony, as well developing The Drugs Don't Work. During this period, he also wrote what would become A Song for The Lovers and C'Mon People, songs later completed for his first solo album.

Free of the distractions of band politics, it was Ashcroft's most productive period as a songwriter. Emboldened, in March 1996 Ashcroft played his first solo slot, supporting Oasis at The Paramount in New York. Armed only with his acoustic guitar, he gave live debuts to Sonnet, Space and Time and The Drugs Don't Work.

Back in Bath, John Leckie, the producer of *A Storm in Heaven,* happened to be working nearby at the Real World Studios and, upon hearing the demos, urged Ashcroft to record the new material for his solo career. With Tong, Jones and Salisbury ably providing instrumentation, the collective demoed a total of 32 tracks, a mixture of Ashcroft compositions and more jam-based songs, in line with The Verve's approach. Alas, despite the addition of the versatile Tong, the music was missing the flourishes that Ashcroft felt the songs warranted.

One of his chosen options for a replacement for McCabe was John Squire, the recently departed guitarist from The Stone Roses. Squire, a founding member of the seminal band, had left the Roses in spring 1996, citing the old favourite of 'musical differences.' Upon meeting Squire at a party, Ashcroft reportedly proposed the idea of joining his new band to the guitarist, who briefly accepted the offer but soon withdrew as he had his own project in mind. His project was a four-piece that would go on to become The Seahorses. Coincidentally, Nick McCabe's name was in the frame to replace Squire in his former band.

Continuing to look for his own Keith Richards, Ashcroft then approached former Suede guitarist Bernard Butler. On the surface, it seemed like a good fit, with Butler having had the experience of working in a tempestuous band environment, but once again the idea failed to get any traction. Butler spent a week with Ashcroft and co, creating what he would later describe as 'amazing sounds', but ultimately it was agreed to part ways amicably.

The search for a producer was equally fruitless. The sessions with Leckie came up short, as did another go with Owen Morris. Ashcroft spent two weeks at Rockfield Studios with the Welsh producer, but the sessions produced nothing. Both Morris and Ashcroft cited the sessions for *A Northern Soul* as incredibly stressful, indeed they were reported to be partially responsible for the singer's decision to quit the Verve, so it was hardly surprising when Ashcroft returned from Wales empty-handed. At the recommendation of John Best, Ashcroft approached Youth.

Youth (aka Martin Glover) was a founding member of rock band Killing Joke who had successfully moved into music production. By the late-1990s he had produced work by PJ Harvey and U2, as well as forming a duo with Paul McCartney, called The Fireman. Designed as an outlet for McCartney to embrace his electronic avant-garde leanings, the pair had released an ambient album in 1993 to critical acclaim, despite the identities of the two men being an open secret (McCartney wishing to keep the project anonymous as an experiment).

Youth's professionalism was valued by Ashcroft, as the producer urged him to adopt a more classic, song-based approach while also trimming away the more indulgent elements of the music. Given his wholehearted commitment and dedication to his new project, Ashcroft was more than happy to oblige. Youth also talked the young singer out of abandoning one of the main demos, a lament called Bitter Sweet Symphony.

Having picked up a copy of an album called *The Rolling Stones Songbook,* Ashcroft's ears had pricked when he heard an orchestral version of The Last Time made by the Stones' manager Andrew Loog Oldham, credited to The Andrew Oldham Orchestra. The *Songbook* album had been Oldham's attempt to prove that Jagger/Richards was one of the greatest song writing partnerships in history, and as such their work could be applied to any genre without diminishing the quality of the song itself.

Ashcroft had taken a loop from the orchestral version containing the sounds of strings and bells, then built the rest of his own song, Bitter Sweet Symphony, around it, with Will Malone once again adding further strings. Looping a sample for a song was a technique favoured by hip-hop artists but had not, at this point, been a prominent approach taken by rock bands. Ashcroft was convinced that it could be 'turned into something outrageous.'

All involved decamped to Olympic Studios in West London to record, but while the studio tapes for the sessions were labelled 'Richard Ashcroft', Youth frequently wrote 'The Verve' on the studio boards, with Ashcroft having to correct him every time. Despite there being three members of The Verve involved, as far as Ashcroft was concerned, it was a separate entity without Nick McCabe. Despite their grievances, Ashcroft knew that McCabe's contributions were a huge part of the band and to pretend otherwise was misleading and disrespectful. Although the collective didn't have a name, the album they were working on did: *Urban Hymns.*

The (near) wholesale changes also applied to the management; disenfranchised with Savage and Best,

Ashcroft dispensed with their services to work with Jazz Summers, a British manager who had previously worked with Wham! While it may not have been an obvious fit, with very few (alright, no) similarities between George Michael and Andrew Ridgeley's pop behemoth and the psychedelic, widescreen guitar rock that Ashcroft et al had delivered, the singer appreciated how successful Wham! had been in breaking America, and perhaps fancied some of that commercial nous would help him break into the mainstream. Summers also came up with the idea of making Wham! the first western act to perform in the lucrative market of China.

Simon Tong explains in the notes for the deluxe edition of *Urban Hymns* that the sessions were positive, 'The label was very supportive. They poured a lot of money into the development of what would become *Urban Hymns*. That gave us the freedom to piss about in the studio and work out what it was we wanted to do. But from a very early point, you could tell that there was something special there. There was momentum. The first two records hadn't sold that well but there was a lot of love for them in different circles, here and in America as well. They'd turned a lot of people's heads. There was a definite feeling that this was going to explode at some point. We all felt very confident.' (xxx)

Meanwhile, back in Wigan, Nick McCabe was in a bad way. Although he had joined another band after his departure from The Verve, he had already given up on it and was resigned to not being a professional musician at all. He was watching from afar as the band he was a founder of moved from under him. Although he made some home recordings himself, McCabe was focused on working with his daughter's mother to bring up their child as separated parents. His friends were concerned for his well-being as he suffered from depression, even going so far as to try and have the erstwhile guitarist sectioned at Christmas 1996. McCabe had heard from Jones and

Salisbury but had not seen or heard from Richard Ashcroft since the split over a year earlier, so it was surely quite a surprise to receive a phone call from Ashcroft on New Year's Day 1997, asking McCabe if he would re-join The Verve.

Ashcroft had been thinking about McCabe for some time. He was caught in a dilemma of having written some great songs, having artistic and creative freedom in being the driving force of whatever this project was but knowing (or rather feeling) that something was missing and more could be done. Having ignored the voices telling him to contact McCabe, eventually he snapped and picked up the phone, although he had many opportunities to change his mind as McCabe was hard to track down. When they eventually did speak, Ashcroft, characteristically dramatically, told McCabe he would quit music altogether if the elder man did not take up his offer. The guitarist had made peace with the fact that his ejection from the band was partly his fault and was, therefore, able to accept Ashcroft's offer with the grace it deserved, although he did say to the singer, 'Y'know, I should tell you to fuck off.' (xxxi)

It was a very gallant gesture from Ashcroft, although he was surely wise to the fact that The Verve would perform better in a commercial sense than a solo Richard Ashcroft (or whatever other name he could come up with). Additionally, The Verve were four distinct but equally important parts and were most certainly worth another crack at world domination. But all the emotions involved with the band were put to one side, as McCabe reflects in the *Urban Hymns* boxset notes: 'As with everything Verve-related there was strict avoidance of the elephant in the room – I'd been sacked and reinstated, but for the sake of the music I just got on with it. Dysfunction as per usual.' (xxxii)

And so, how to put McCabe to work? Asking Simon Tong to leave not long after he had joined was unnecessary, as his ability to contribute on keys or as a rhythm guitarist was useful. He could only add to their epic tendencies. The idea of re-recording 15 songs from scratch was also an extreme reaction given how far into recording Ashcroft, Jones, Salisbury, and Tong were. Instead, the now quintet referred to their default method of creativity: expression via unrestrained jamming. Catching the Butterfly and Weeping Willow were two of six new songs that came out of the jamming, as was the last track recorded for the album, Neon Wilderness.

'We were the Verve again. It was like we'd played the week before together. It was beautiful and natural,' (xxxiii) says Simon Jones in the *Urban Hymns* notes. It's not unreasonable to speculate that McCabe and Tong may not have worked well together in the band, the new boy ostensibly being McCabe's replacement, but he had nothing but praise for Tong, 'I loved playing with Tongy. There was most mutual respect between us and since he was a solid technical player where I deferred to spontaneity, it meant that I didn't have to be mindful of supporting the structure.' (xxxiv)

For a while, the concoction was perfect. With Youth's guidance Ashcroft had set out the template of the album, adhering more to song structures than anything else. Individually the parts were added, with McCabe adding icing on the cake with his creative, spontaneous, and unique guitar playing. With McCabe's confidence rising due to being asked back, the stars were aligning.

Throughout the recording, Youth had gradually transferred production responsibilities to engineer Chris Potter and departed the project entirely just before Christmas 1996. That did not seem to affect the sessions or momentum, and in February 1997, The Verve dusted down and recorded some outstanding tracks from the *A Northern Soul* sessions, The Rolling People and Come On. The clock was starting to tick, with money invested by the label and the studio time taking up over a year, but it didn't seem to influence or distract the band, such was their belief in the record.

Of utmost importance was the comeback single. It had to announce that this band of waifs and strays were to be taken seriously. It had to be a big statement. It had to be Bitter Sweet Symphony.

Single 9:

Bitter Sweet Symphony
Released: 16 June 1997; UK Chart Position: 2; Label: Hut Recordings; Album: *Urban Hymns*
Track Listing: CD1: Bitter Sweet Symphony (original); Lord I Guess I'll Never Know; Country Song**; Bitter Sweet Symphony (radio edit)
CD2: Bitter Sweet Symphony (extended version); So Sister*; Echo Bass*
Producers: Youth/The Verve; *Chris Potter/The Verve; **Owen Morris/Chris Potter/The Verve
Bitter Sweet Symphony by Jagger/Richards (lyrics by Richard Ashcroft). Lord I Guess I'll Never Know and So Sister written by Richard Ashcroft.

Ashcroft's original intention was to create a track that would sit alongside the classic Ennio Morricone scores for the spaghetti western movies of the 1970s, but the idea evolved into a Phil Spector, wall of sound-style approach. After adding layer upon layer of tracks to the mix, the final mix ended up with 47 tracks (including the famous string refrain which was written by The Verve) which buried the original sample further.

As was standard practice, before the single's release The Verve's management team approached the copyright holders of the sample track and negotiated the rights to use a six-note sample from Decca Records. However, they failed to get permission from ABKCO

(The Allen and Betty Klein Company). Allen Klein was one of the most infamous managers in rock and held the unique achievement of managing both The Rolling Stones and The Beatles at the same point. He was also a notoriously tough person to deal with. In 1971 Paul McCartney had to issue a writ to dissolve The Beatles to break free of Klein's financial clutches, while The Rolling Stones relinquished $15 million of missing money and the copyright to every song they had recorded in the 1960s.

Shortly before the release, ABKCO informed The Verve's new manager Jazz Summers that they were refusing clearance of the sample. Taking matters into his own hands, the manager contacted the American branch of Virgin records for help, whose vice-chairman contacted both Mick Jagger and Keith Richards. Nancy Berry played the track to the Glimmer Twins, with both reportedly liking the track but refusing to get involved in the dispute, aware that any participation would involve re-engaging with Klein.

With the possibility of a likely hit single having to go unreleased, The Verve and their management team were distraught. Obviously aware of the position he was putting them in, Allen Klein stated his proposed terms of a 50/50 split of the royalties which, in fairness, was standard practice for sampled material. Relieved, plans for the release date recommenced until Klein contacted Summers to clarify what he meant by 50/50; 50% for Jagger, 50% for Richards. By then, it was far too late to change anything, which Allen Klein would surely have known.

Bitter Sweet Symphony was released with the credits listed as: 'Performed by the Andrew Oldham Orchestra. Produced by Andrew Loog Oldham of the Decca record company limited. Vocals by Richard Ashcroft. Bitter Sweet Symphony written by Mick Jagger and Keith Richards. Published by ABKCO Music Inc. Lyrics by Richard Ashcroft.' Convoluted, to say the least.

The relevance of the lyric 'you're a slave to money then you die' was not lost on the frontman.

Ironically, The Last Time was influenced by a song of the same name by American Gospel outfit The Staple Singers. Their version had the same tune and the same riff but with different lyrics, and so when The Rolling Stones pilfered it there were no consequences, mainly because people simply did not sue in the early days of the music industry. The Verve were snookered. To pull the plug on the single's release would now cost them money, and they stood to make no money in royalties from it. They were in the unusual position of being caught between wanting their best song to perform well but not *too* well. A smash hit might be too hard to stomach, although given that The Verve had never broken the top 10, it was unlikely to be too much of a problem.

Over-exposure may have dulled its power, but not by much. Bitter Sweet Symphony is still one of the most remarkable pieces of music of the 20th century, let alone the 1990s (it regularly receives various accolades of that nature). The evocative opening strings, as they build and build until the drums kick in, are life-affirming and hit that sweet spot in the listener's subconscious that makes the ears prick and the hairs stand up on end. Its author's description of it as a 'modern-day blues song' is incredibly accurate. It laments the rigours and travails of contemporary life while tapping into the human feeling ('I'm a million different people from one day to the next, I can't change my mould') and aptly capturing the power of music ('I let the melody shine, let it cleanse my mind, I feel free now') while Tong and McCabe complement each other perfectly. One of those beautiful, infrequent moments in life when public opinion and critical reception are in simpatico, made even more remarkable by the fact that, yet again, there is no real chorus to cling to. In 2004, it was ranked at number 392 on *Rolling Stone*'s list of 'The 500 Greatest Songs of All Time' and according to Acclaimed Music, it is the 59th most celebrated song in popular music history. (xxxv)

In the *Urban Hymns* deluxe edition notes, Ashcroft provided some further details on the subject matter, 'It's about modern-day slavery and no matter how much you think you're free in your mind, even as a musician, there's always something pulling you back, necessitating you, forcing you to work in some guise to bring the food home, to pay the bills, to get the guy off your back…ultimately the dream was to do something that had that impact to prove it could still be done – that something incredibly popular could be well designed. The mantra seemed to be that those times were done. They'd all happened in the 1950s or 60s or 70s. These peaks could never be reached again.' (xxxvi)

The B-sides across the two CDs are a good encapsulation of where The Verve were at this point. Lord I Guess I'll Never Know is a grandiose number of the kind on *Urban Hymns*, but with less scope within the song to push it like the rest, although a sumptuous bass delivery by Simon Jones accompanies an Ashcroft now confidently showing off his vocal range. So Sister is built around the singer and acoustic guitar (although McCabe or Tong are plotting away in the background) and is a stark lost gem. The other two tracks are band workouts; the spiky western blues track Country Song is overly long, like some of the first album material, with a telling lyric ('these are my times') that perhaps reflects Ashcroft's justified self-confidence at this point. On the battering funk of Echo Bass Ashcroft uses his voice as an instrument, both baritone and falsetto working well in conjunction with one another.

How frustrated The Verve, and specifically Richard Ashcroft, must have been on that Sunday as Bitter Sweet Symphony reached number 2 in the UK singles chart. His belief had paid off and the band had finally smashed through into the mainstream, but the song credits debacle cast a cloud over its success. The epitome of a first-world problem but a genuine source of ire, nonetheless.

The performance of the song can only have been assisted by its iconic video, with which it now has a symbiotic relationship. In a leather jacket that was far too big for his thin frame, it featured Ashcroft walking down Hoxton Street in East London, as he walked past and often through passers-by before being joined by the rest of the band (Simon Tong slotting in easily) at the end, as if to emphasise that it was, in a designed way, Richard Ashcroft and the others. It segues into The Drugs Don't Work video and has a nod to their past, flashing the band logo used from *No Come Down* against a vending machine from which one could buy feelings. Much parodied since, not least by Fat Les for their 1998 World Cup song Vindaloo a year later, the video was devised by director Walter Stern as a homage to the iconic single continuous shot video for Massive Attack's Unfinished Sympathy. The video received heavy rotation on all the major music channels.

Although 1994-1996 is viewed as peak Britpop and 1997 is regarded as the year the wheels started to come off, in terms of chart success, 1997 was the scene's zenith. Blur, Cast and Ocean Colour Scene (the latter pair regarded as the second wave of Britpop) all occupied the top 10, but none of them could get near Puff Daddy & Faith Evans' I'll Be Missing You, a tribute to the Notorious B.I.G. who had been murdered in March 1997.

Built around the bassline from Every Breath You Take by The Police, it was the third biggest-selling UK single of the year and spent a total of six weeks at the top slot. (xxxvii) Only the mighty Oasis, with their comeback single D'You Know What I Mean? were able to knock it off the top slot and even then, only for one week before it reclaimed the position. A behemoth for the year. Bitter Sweet Symphony, therefore, joins Common People and Wonderwall as timeless British pop songs that just came up short, but have more than stood the test of time and outlasted the tracks that stood in their way. The Verve's nemeses are not in the same category as Robson & Jerome, however, who kept both Oasis and Pulp at bay.

Regardless, The Verve were now pop stars and their experiences with Allen Klein became public knowledge. Ashcroft was understandably glib (among other emotions he was undoubtedly experiencing), describing his masterpiece as 'the best song Jagger and Richards have written in 20 years.'

CHAPTER FIVE
'This Could be My Moment, Something More Than Weather' (1997)

As was becoming a pattern for The Verve and their members, good news would soon be followed by bad. A comeback tour, which would have undoubtedly been triumphant given where the band were, had to be cancelled because of Richard Ashcroft's ill health, which stemmed from viral problems. At points unable to sing, he was advised by his doctor to take six weeks off work. The tour would have been the first live outings for The Verve in two years.

Speaking to the *NME*, Ashcroft was sanguine on the matter, 'I never got to the point where I was truly up for it, to be honest. For one, I was in the middle of finishing the record, so you've got to look after your energy levels, and two, I was very ill. Everyone else apart from me was gagging for it…whatever it takes wasn't there. And what we do is just too big to go out there as anything less than 100%.' (xxxviii) This all-or-nothing attitude had been with the band since the start and showed no signs of diminishing, despite their now celebrated status.

The music press had further Verve-related copy in June 1997, as Spiritualized released their seminal album *Ladies and Gentlemen We Are Floating in Space.* A mournful, funereal album seemingly built on heartbreak, it was decided that Jason Pierce was baring his soul and eulogising about his former relationship with Kate Radley, with the media picking up on album tracks Broken Heart and Cool Waves as prime examples. Pierce denied the claims, pointing out that both tracks were written before he and Radley separated, but by then the damage was done.

When The Verve were finally able to tour, they exorcised some demons by performing History for the first time, including it in a set that was heavy on *A Northern Soul* material alongside a handful of the forthcoming songs. The tour included a slot at Reading Festival, headlining the *Melody Maker* stage. In the run-up to the release of *Urban Hymns*, a second single was released in early September – The Drugs Don't Work.

Single 10:

The Drugs Don't Work
Released: 1 September 1997; UK Chart Position: 1;
Label: Hut Recordings; Album: *Urban Hymns*
Track Listing: CD1: The Drugs Don't Work (radio edit); Three Steps**; The Drugs Don't Work (demo)
CD2: The Drugs Don't Work; Bitter Sweet Symphony (James Lavelle Remix); The Crab*; Stamped**
Producers: Youth/The Verve; *John Leckie/Chris Potter/The Verve; **Potter/The Verve
The Drugs Don't Work and The Crab written by Richard Ashcroft. Three Steps written by Ashcroft/Jones/McCabe/Salisbury/Tong.

It's now lost on the mists of time, or more likely buried under the omnipresence of the song, but The Drugs Don't Work was controversial in autumn 1997, namely because of the title. Although Ashcroft preferred the lyrics to be ambiguous, it was rumoured that the song was about his father and the grief involved during his last days. However, it is worth pointing out that back in 1995 the singer had mentioned the track and implicitly referred to his drug intake. The truth probably lies somewhere in between the two theories, but only Richard Ashcroft can say. The Drugs Don't Work was one of the tunes which were fully formed by the time McCabe re-joining the band,

and his guitar parts were the added flourishes (recorded in one take) that prevented the song from becoming too mawkish.

The Chart Show banned the video because of the content (although to be fair, the show was aired on Saturday mornings) and the directness of the title raised eyebrows, despite its surface-level anti-drug message. Ashcroft had asked the programme's makers to run the video without their trademark captions on screen, which surely made their decision easier. Not that a bit of controversy ever hurt a pop single, which was later nominated for a prestigious Ivor Novello award in its 'Song of The Year' category. (xxxix)

If 'pop' can be a suitable description for this layered, emotionally charged and lusciously produced piece of music. The structure is key; the strings fade in and then signpost every tonal change flagrantly, yet it makes the transition the more satisfying. Each instrument is introduced incrementally as the rest of the band very much takes a back seat to Ashcroft. As with much of its parent album, The Drugs Don't Work is drenched in vocal harmonies, some of which are only heard once as if to tease the listener that the possibilities of the song are endless. Unashamedly tugging at the heartstrings, its sincerity is its strength.

Three Steps is a rollicking tonic from the heartbreak, an alternative version of Come On played at a different tempo with a fresh melody and lyrics, further evidence of the influence of looping and technology was having on the band. The Crab is another stark acoustic track made atmospheric via some steel guitar but outstays its welcome at nearly six minutes, while the instrumental Stamped is Pink Floydian at the beginning before becoming a band workout featuring some splendid drum fills by Salisbury.

The singles offered a couple of alternative versions; the demo of the title track offers some alternative lyrics which are a good marker of the song's evolution, while the bass-heavy James Lavelle remix of 'Bitter Sweet Symphony' cuts the song down to its core, and it is only when the strings come in halfway through that you realise that they weren't there before.

Like Wonderwall before it, The Drugs Don't Work is undeniably one of the most influential songs of the era. Depending on your point of view, it was either the high-water mark or it has a lot to answer for. The roots of the string-laden, well-produced moving anthems that would become the default setting for British indie for several years were laid here, with a heart-on-sleeve honesty and vulnerability that even appealed to alpha-males. Travis, Coldplay and Starsailor were paying close attention.

The Drugs Don't Work was released the day after Princess Diana died in Paris and hit the number 1 slot six days later. Many writers and observers conclude that The Verve were fortuitous enough to tap into the public mood and, while it is a reasonable assumption to make, it seems unlikely that the sort of people who were buying singles by The Verve in the first week of release were hugely affected by her death. Indeed, one week later the Princess Diana tribute single, a re-recorded Candle in The Wind by Elton John, obviously designed for such a purpose, toppled The Verve from their perch.

Whether or not the comparison is true, The Verve (along with Radiohead and Spiritualized) were beneficiaries of a change in the musical wind. Gone was the thirst for bravado and braggadocio. More nuance and melancholy were required to reflect the more sombre mood as the UK approached the millennium. While Radiohead had captured the pre-millennial anxiety on *OK Computer*, released earlier in the summer of 1997, The Verve had taken the everyman quality (and to a lesser extent, the anthemic aspirations) of Oasis but lined it with more melancholic delivery.

But their kinship with Oasis had continued and the Mancunians invited The Verve to play as very special guests at three huge indoor shows at London's Earls Court towards the end of September. While The Verve were having their time, following the release of the overblown *Be Here Now*, Oasis were slipping out of step with their audience and British music, slowly but surely. The Earls Court shows were only a month after the release of their third album and the tide was yet to turn. As such, the music media seemed determined to set the gigs up as a 'Battle of the Bands', despite their friendship. Their attempts were in vain, with Oasis dedicating D'You Know What I Mean? to The Verve. But it was testament to how important the Wigan quintet were becoming that the comparisons were being made in the first place.

Album 3:

Urban Hymns
Released: 29 September 1997; UK Chart Position: 1; Label: Hut Recordings
Track Listing: Bitter Sweet Symphony; Sonnet; The Rolling People*; The Drugs Don't Work; Catching the Butterfly*; Neon Wilderness*; Space and Time*; Weeping Willow*; Lucky Man; One Day; This Time; Velvet Morning; Come On* (includes hidden song Deep Freeze)
Producers: Youth/The Verve; *Chris Potter/The Verve
All songs written by Richard Ashcroft except The Rolling People, Catching the Butterfly and Come On written by The Verve. Neon Wilderness written by The Verve and Nick McCabe.

An instantly recognisable cover image of the band sitting in Richmond Park (Ashcroft, Salisbury, Jones, and Tong looking to their right, McCabe to his left) soon became iconic, and later launched a thousand memes in 2020. Social distancing rules due to the COVID pandemic meant that, following a national lockdown, people would be able to congregate in small numbers in parks or other outdoor areas. See what they did there?

For those that love a conspiracy theory, McCabe looking in the opposite direction represented his previous (and future) ostracization from the band. He stood apart. The interior artwork included a letter from Andrew Loog Oldham where he stated that he loved Bitter Sweet Symphony and that 'the Stones were probably too old to remember where they nicked that particular riff from themselves.' Richard Ashcroft would refuse to stay silent about the saga and was determined that people would regard the song as his, even if the copyright and credits said otherwise.

Urban Hymns was released on 29 September 1997 and, with two hit singles preceding it, hit the number 1 slot, displacing *Be Here Now* in the process in a symbolic changing of the guard. More unexpected was the ferocity of the sales: 750,000 units (xl) were shifted in its first week and over seven million worldwide. At the time of writing, it still occupies a place in the UK best-selling albums of all time (19), and it rises to 13 once compilations are removed.

Elsewhere in the album chart, *Be Here Now* had begun its fall from grace and dropped three places, while Ocean Colour Scene were at the peak of their commercial success with *Marchin' Already*. Elsewhere in the top 10, the old guard was well-represented with new albums by The Rolling Stones, Bob Dylan and Elton John featuring prominently (although the latter surely received a fillip from Candle in The Wind '97's success), while *OK Computer* and *The Fat of The Land* by The Prodigy, another alternative music success story, sat just outside. Interestingly, given the success it would later go on to achieve, Robbie Williams' debut album, *Life Thru A Lens*, entered the charts at number 11. This was before the release of Angels and Let Me Entertain You. *Urban Hymns* sat at the top of the charts for five weeks, until The Spice Girls' sophomore effort usurped it, but it performed well for the remainder of the year. (xli)

Although it's undeniably primarily the work of Richard Ashcroft (who now considers it to be his first solo album), *Urban Hymns* is a collaborative piece. The Rolling People was a few years old upon its release and, ironically considering their previous barbs against them, channels U2 in its persistent verse which then slides into a big chorus. It riffs on Four Horsemen by Aphrodite's Child as Nick McCabe is unashamedly kissing the sky and it would have been nice to hear his work in full glory, but Ashcroft douses the whole song in vocals as if refusing to be dominated. Such was the balance of power within the band at the time. The last, unexpected bang of the drum as the song concludes reflects the band playing tricks on the listener as if to demonstrate their power and hold over us.

The pulsing bass of Catching the Butterfly claws at the psyche with an Eastern tilt and best demonstrates the increased clarity in the production, as provided by Chris Potter, with excellent shuffling drumming by Pete Salisbury, while on the gargantuan Come On (which owes a debt to Crime and the City Solution's Stone) McCabe unleashes his inner Hendrix. It is a righteous, unholy rock and roll song and a call-to-arms ('I never met no-one to deny our sound') with which Liam Gallagher (drafted in to provide backing for the outro) cannot compete, indiscernible from the tornado of noise surrounds him. It's probably still going, somewhere out in space. The remaining band composition, Neon Wilderness, is a throwback to their days as sonic adventurers and was fittingly the last track recorded in the sessions, at 7 am on the last studio day allocated to them. There was no better way to complete the circle.

The rest of the tracks are listed as Ashcroft compositions and, while it is unfair to see it as his first solo album, there is a distinct lineage to his solo career. Space and Time was apparently Liam Gallagher's favourite and it is not hard to see why, being like Oasis in its execution, structure, and musicianship. The matter-of-fact verse gives way to some back-and-forth vocals on the bridge, taking the song to another level before a simple but uplifting chorus, while Salisbury ladens the song with fills. Weeping Willow is all menace and mood, the sound of envy and lust put to music but offset by the lyrics which, like much else, cover love and life. The winsome One Day is one song that could have been removed but it is undoubtedly someone's favourite Verve song, and its main issue is the strength of the surrounding competition. It does sail close to the wind of pastiche ('One day maybe you will love again') but is held back by the proficiency of the band. In contrast, This Time is tribal dance music, as Ashcroft pushes himself by rapping heavenly on the verse. It is a lament on one's past and has the maturity of a writer in his fifties, not aged 24/25 as Ashcroft was when he wrote it. Another precursor to his solo work but delivered by more innovative musicians.

Meanwhile, the majestic Velvet Morning near enough puts the listener through the gamut of emotions its recalling. It rises and lifts with a heart-breaking moment at the 'Don't you find' section. Singing the verse through a loudhailer, Ashcroft wrenches every emotion from the song. It takes its cue from Some Velvet Morning by Lee Hazelwood (later covered by Primal Scream & Kate Moss), but in its build to a cathartic outro, it should be held at least partially responsible for Snow Patrol's early 21st-century output. On the CD version, the album closes after a long pause with a dystopian noise entitled Deep Freeze, featuring a baby crying, and was quite disturbing to hear if you had drifted off to sleep listening to the album, surely by design.

Urban Hymns is, like its lead single, one of those beautiful moments in life when everything clicks. Production, musical proficiency, songs, and confidence all gel, but with an underlying sadness which, in Britain, was a real insight into the mood of the country in the immediate aftermath of Princess Diana's death. The good times hadn't been forgotten but now they were tempered with sorrow, with everyone either having felt it or been exposed to it. Given what we know, there can be little doubt that Nick McCabe mainly added to it rather than created it. Not that he takes a backseat but there is so much more going on around him by this point. Some minutes are wasted but no time is and even now, more than two decades on, it still reveals something new on each listen.

Several other tracks were recorded over the same period as *Urban Hymns* which only saw the light of day some years later. This Could Be My Moment and Monte Carlo later went on 2004's best of *This is Music,* but a further eleven tracks were leaked online after the deluxe boxset in 2017, including alternative or demo versions of This Time, Sonnet and Neon Wilderness as well as an alternative Deep Freeze, rechristened Original Insanity. Seven original tracks were also found, Sweet & Sour is chunky, percussion-heavy, and meditative but a bit rudderless (and rumoured to be an early version of Bitter Sweet Symphony), Wednesday Madness perhaps recalls the *A Northern Soul* days (in that Wednesday would be the only day any work would be done) and is a largely aimless instrumental.

Jalfrezi has a subtle, muted joy with a gorgeous melody. Tina Turner (a song title) has shades of Albatross by Peter Green's Fleetwood Mac, Oh Sister is a straightforward swashbuckling rocker with a strong chorus but little else, and King Riff 2 rattles the bones with clatters of cymbals and electric guitar. The best of the bunch is All Ways Are Maybes, a fully formed, sweeping number which is surely due a re-appraisal by its composer but, like all the tracks, has its strengths but was perhaps deemed too similar other tracks on *Urban Hymns* to fly. For whatever reason, Ashcroft exercised his veto, and the tracks were not included on the special edition.

The sales of the album were aided by the positive reviews it received. *Melody Maker* called it 'an album of unparalleled beauty' while the *NME* compared it, inevitably, to Oasis but with a twist, Ted Kessler declaring that 'it finally carves The Verve's name alongside that of their Mancunian peers in history's grand ledger. It insists, however, that they will be the ones writing the next chapter.' (xlii) The positive reviews weren't confined to the UK, as *Rolling Stone* called it 'a breath-taking venture, an ambitious balance of stargazing and worldly pathos.' (xliii) For once, with the stars finally aligned, The Verve could look to the future with renewed confidence and positivity. That future involved a world tour in 1998, the tickets for which (in Europe) sold out within two hours.

CHAPTER SIX
'He Was Restless, Escape Loneliness, Find a New Address' (1997-99)

With Bitter Sweet Symphony firmly lodged in the US Modern Rock chart, aided by the heavy rotation of the track on MTV, The Verve followed up their Earl's Court dates with twelve dates across America which, for once, went without a hitch. Back home, a third single was lifted from *Urban Hymns* in November 1997, Lucky Man.

Single 11:

Lucky Man
Released: 24 November 1997; UK Chart Position: 7;
Label: Hut Recordings; Album: *Urban Hymns*
B-sides: CD1: Never Wanna See You Cry**; History
CD2: MSG; The Longest Day*; Lucky Man (Happiness More or Less)
Producer: Youth/The Verve; *Chris Potter/The Verve
All tracks written by Richard Ashcroft, except MSG (Jagger/Richards) and The Longest Day written by Ashcroft/Jones/McCabe/Salisbury.

On an album crammed with classics, Lucky Man is still one of the standout tracks. Built around four chords, it draws itself into the listener rather than the other way round. In terms of the structure of simplicity, it's the closest Richard Ashcroft ever came to writing Wonderwall. With an emotive bridge that carries the melody into a righteous chorus that can be sung or shouted easily, it is perhaps The Verve's definitive 'everyman' anthem. Its key strength is in Will Malone's sweeping strings which drive it and make it not only transcendent but also one of the songs of the 1990s that Bono wishes he had written. (xliv) Make of that what you will.

The video, shot in the Thames Reach development in Hammersmith, is joyous in its way but features Ashcroft performing to what is essentially an audience of four (i.e., the band) who nod along gamely, Pete doing his bit with the tambourine. The B-sides do carry an air of barrel-scraping, Never Wanna See You Cry is overly sentimental, the sort of song that can be played at a funeral (and a real glimpse of the future for Ashcroft), and The Longest Day is a forgettable wander down some blind alleys.

MSG is another alternate version of Bitter Sweet Symphony, lifting the percussion and bass and transplanting into a psychedelic, shimmering soundscape, while Happiness More Or Less was a rush job by Nick McCabe to fill a slot on the track list. It is the same song as the A-side, minus vocals, and guitars. The inclusion of History (probably an attempt to divert the new fans to previous work) adds to the impression that releasing the single over two CDs was unnecessary. Yet the approach was a success as Lucky Man was the third single in a row to hit the top 10, coming in at number 7, and it capped off The Verve's most successful year.

As befitting their new status, the Verve's gigs were more spread out and in January 1998 they put on five gigs across the UK at three venues in Glasgow, Manchester, and London, the three musical lynchpins of the nation, which were followed by two of the key musical awards ceremonies. The first was the *NME* awards where they unsurprisingly cleaned up, winning Best Band, Best Video and Best Single (both for Bitter Sweet Symphony) all of which were announced by host Eddie Izzard.

In what looked like a show of arrogance, the band did not get on stage to collect the awards and instead they were handed them by *NME* editor Steve Sutherland in one fell swoop. However, the band were told at the beginning of the ceremony that they would be receiving four awards and were determined not to make people cringe at three different acceptance speeches, full of meaningless platitudes or attention-seeking soundbites. In the press room afterward, Ashcroft clarified the apparent confusion and went on to confirm that the awards did mean something to them, as they were those voted for by the people who fully appreciated artists: fans and journalists. There was also the risk of the over-exposure that their recent stratospheric success was bound to come with.

The following week it was the turn of the more industry-friendly Brit Awards. Despite being nominated for five awards and winning three (Best British Group, Album of The Year and Producer of The Year with Youth and Chris Potter), The Verve were notable by their absence, the glamour, and the glitz of the Brit Awards not their style. Instead, they were back at Brixton Academy playing a gig as part of a charity event for *The Big Issue* and the homelessness charity Youth2000. They did allow their performance of Lucky Man to be shown as part of the Brit event, although their arm was surely twisted by the Brits arranging for Ashcroft's childhood hero, footballer George Best, to present their awards.

The former Manchester United footballer was not the only iconic figure from days gone by praising the band. Ex-Zombie Rod Argent, composer of the sixties classic She's Not There compared The Verve to The Beatles, 'they're stretching pop boundaries and not writing simple love songs. The Beatles created a consciousness in the general public that was eager for boundaries to be broken,' while Robert Planet was heard to comment, 'I think *A Northern Soul* is brilliant', although his song writing partner Jimmy Page wasn't quite so up-to-date, confusing The Verve for Blur. Best of all, considering the song-based approach that Ashcroft and co. were moving towards, was patronage from The Kinks' Ray Davies, the architect of numerous classic pop singles, 'I love the record and I've got the album. I play it a lot. I like them as an acoustic act, the stuff I've seen him doing unplugged. I think that's quite interesting.' (xlv)

Surprisingly, The Verve's media presence during the *Urban Hymns* campaign was sparse in comparison to previous albums, perhaps due to their reticence to over-exposing themselves. That changed in March 1998 when they (well, Ashcroft) were given an illustrious cover feature for *Rolling Stone* to accompany a wide-reaching interview with the band, apart from Nick McCabe (who was participating in a personal press embargo) and Simon Tong. The feature piece went into detail about McCabe, with Simon Jones and Dan Boyd offering their insights into the guitarist, but the most cryptic comment came from Ashcroft, 'Me and Nick are more alike than anyone knows.' (xlvi)

The Bitter Sweet Symphony debacle still rankled with Ashcroft, who would give his side of the story to anyone who would listen, 'We sampled four bars. (The riff) was on one track. Then we did forty-seven tracks of music beyond that little piece. We've got our own string players, our own percussion on it. Guitars. We're talking about a four-bar sample turning into Bitter Sweet Symphony – and they're still claiming it's the same song.... it's beyond hip-hop, what we've done. With hip-hop now, the trend is to leave the thing they've sampled as the hook to sell more records. This was old-school hip-hop – take something but really twist it and fuck it up into something else. Take it and use your imagination.' (xlvii)

Ashcroft's irritation was understandable, but in the spring of 1998, he was able to chalk up one moral victory against Klein. Nike approached ABKCO with the idea of using the Andrew Loog Oldham version of The Last Time (now given a new lease of life) for a campaign for sneakers. The money-driven Klein readily accepted. But after finalising their deal with Allen Klein, Nike also approached Jazz Summers on the off chance, knowing that their audience would associate the song with The Verve anyway, and talked the manager into it. Summers, in turn, sold the idea to his clients and a deal was agreed to use Bitter Sweet Symphony for the campaign, which saw The Verve gain $700,000 for the pleasure. To their immense credit, they donated the fee to the Red Cross Landmines Appeal and Youth 2000, the homelessness project they had supported for the gig in Brixton.

Although Ashcroft was despondent about the commercialisation of his masterpiece ('The last thing in the world I wanted was for one of my songs to be used in a commercial. I'm still sick about it,'), the advert played its part as sales of *Urban Hymns* doubled in America, with the increased radio play of Bitter Sweet Symphony ensuring it went up in the singles chart. So, Allen Klein, the man who had swindled The Verve out of their royalties, was now indirectly responsible for setting them on the path to being millionaires through their album sales. If Klein had not been so inflexible over The Last Time sample, Bitter Sweet Symphony would never have even been considered for commercial use as The Verve would have dismissed the idea out of hand. As a result of the ubiquity of Bitter Sweet Symphony, The Verve had to cancel their spring tour of the US to line up larger venues.

The gargantuan success of *Urban Hymns* led to a huge number of their new fans to track down their previous work, and it was surely a shock for someone who was only aware of this perfectly polished, mainstream, human rock band to then expose themselves to the claustrophobic, anxious and, in terms of songcraft, less focussed act of *A Northern Soul* or the wispy dreams of *A Storm in Heaven*. Yet, as reflected in the worldwide album sales, The Verve were picking up new fans at a rapid rate. In a move that was standard industry practice, Hut Recordings requested that a fourth single be lifted from the album to sustain the sales.

They weren't short of options on such a song-heavy album, but the plan hit a snag. The Verve, once again hesitant of over-exposure, refused to sanction the release of a fourth single. Aware of the financial rewards, Hut stood their ground and pushed the band. Eventually, they agreed to release Sonnet as the next single. Their agreement came with a caveat, The Verve insisted on a format that would ensure the second track from *Urban Hymns* would not be eligible for the singles chart (although it still received copious airplay on all the major radio stations). Sonnet was released as part of a set of four 12-inch vinyl records (each containing a different, already released B-side) and limited to only 5000 copies packaged in a cardboard mailer, which could also contain the re-released versions of the previous three singles, to make a unique collector's package. Confusingly, it did receive a CD release shortly afterwards.

Single 12:

Sonnet
Released: 2 March 1998; UK Chart Position: 74; Label: Hut Recordings; Album: *Urban Hymns*
B-sides: Stamped; So Sister; Echo Bass
Producers: Youth/The Verve
Sonnet and So Sister written by Richard Ashcroft.

As anticipated, the plan worked, the UK Official Chart Company refusing to recognise Sonnet as a single because of the extra content. Despite their best intentions, it did eventually scrape into the top 75 because of the sales of an imported format, which was an impressive achievement.

Sonnet features a superlative vocal performance from Richard Ashcroft along with sublime lyrics and, like much of The Verve's work, is devoid of a chorus, instead being a work of three distinct parts that build momentum. The rhythm section is the engine of the song before it pushes skyward. The opening section is Ashcroft, acoustic guitar and piano but the ivories are pushed down the mix by the electric guitar from the second verse onwards. 'Yes, there's love if you want it/don't sound like no sonnet,' acts as the chorus but is little more than a rhyming couplet. The airplay it received ensures it is equally as recognisable to the man in the street as Bitter Sweet Symphony, The Drugs Don't Work and Lucky Man.

In January 1998, The Verve announced a huge homecoming gig at Haigh Hall, just outside the band's native Wigan. The homecoming gig is an opportunity for a band to re-engage with their people after travelling the world. Owing to the understanding relationship between band and crowd (theoretically cut from the same cloth), the atmosphere is always unique, and the bigger the crowd, the better. It was common practice before the 1990s but it became much more symbolic after Blur and Oasis had put on successful shows at London's Mile End Stadium and Maine Road in Manchester, respectively.

The Gallaghers and their merry men would play many more mega-gigs in Manchester throughout their career (including at the City of Manchester Stadium and Heaton Park), but the Maine Road show is always cited as their definitive concert. Indeed, Noel Gallagher claimed that unless you had seen Oasis in Manchester, you haven't really seen them.

When they reformed for some shows in 2009 (and again in 2012 and 2015), Blur played huge open-air gigs at London's Hyde Park (not quite a homecoming but close enough). Following their reunion in 2011, Pulp travelled the world but concluded the run at the Sheffield Arena in late 2012. The Stone Roses made Manchester a priority for their comeback, playing Heaton Park and the City of Manchester stadium as the first shows and then playing in other cities at later dates. It could be argued that a Primal Scream gig only really makes sense in Glasgow.

The newer generations follow the template; Arctic Monkeys played Sheffield's Don Valley Bowl in 2011, Kasabian performed at Leicester's King Power Stadium and Victoria Park at their peak, the Courteeners seem to regularly play Heaton Park…. the list goes on. Having come from the South West, Coldplay and Muse cheat a little by claiming headline slots at Glastonbury as their homecoming gigs. It is a rite of passage for any band and a reference point as to whether the band is 'big' or not.

The Verve's Haigh Hall gig on 24 May 1998 was unique in that it was a once-in-a-lifetime show, but there was some tabloid fodder in the lead-up. Richard Ashcroft's ex-girlfriend, Sarah Carpenter, decided to sell her story to tabloid paper *The Daily Mirror*, sadly a common practice for ex-associates when a band has 'made it'. Carpenter was unlikely to have received anywhere near the amount of money she surely did had she sold her story in 1994, so one can understand the choice from a financial aspect, although the act itself was undignified. Such is the price of fame.

As The Rolling Stones would continually discover, Richard Ashcroft is not one to let things go, and he dealt with the matter in his inimitable fashion. Before performing History at Haigh Hall, he introduced the song by saying, 'To that snidey fucker in the audience who thinks this is about them. Dream on. It's about love and it's about you in the audience making this one of the greatest days of my life.'

The unsavoury incident was the only sour note on what was otherwise a great day. Ashcroft later claimed that it was The Verve's destiny to play the show, citing a conversation he had had with his stepfather, 'Doug visualised the gig at Haigh Hall five years before it happened. He said, 'I can smell the hot dog stands!' I'm not saying it's magic, it's the power of the mind.' (xvc)

As the gig was their own mini-festival, the members of The Verve were able to select their typically eclectic support acts. Whereas Oasis had chosen the acts of the day for their Knebworth shows two years earlier, The Verve were typically less mainstream. The whole band had long been fans of John Martyn, and the Scottish songwriter was first on the bill, followed by pioneer DJ Shadow and then Beck. DJ Shadow used to play History in his DJ sets alongside West Coast hip-hop tracks and had caught Ashcroft's attention, while Beck Hansen had experienced some success of his own with Loser and Devil's Haircut (also remixed by Noel Gallagher). During the latter song, a gang of people without tickets were kicking down the perimeter fence. The police soon regained control, but it was a demonstration of how in-demand tickets for the show were.

The gig was broadcast live on BBC Radio 1 and highlights were shown on BBC television later that night. When they did eventually take to the stage in front of 33,000 gleeful and eager punters, The Verve looked ecstatic, Simon Jones especially. Both he and Ashcroft looked to the crowd and shouted, 'come on!' with the singer simply saying 'This is music' before his band launched into a titanic version of the song of the same name. A statement of fact, an order and song title all summed up in one sentence. Nick McCabe looked every bit the elusive guitarist he was, the wind sweeping through his hair in the dramatic style that the occasion demanded.

Not that he was ever anything else, but by this point, Richard Ashcroft was the ultimate professional. He never missed lyrics, never hit bum notes and, true to his word, never gives anything less than 100%. He may have singled out members of the audience who were rankling him or make scathing comments about certain individuals, but he would never let it affect his performance. Sometimes it would add even more edge. At one point during the show, he accidentally wrapped his microphone cable around the mic stand at the exact point he was about to launch into one of his pointed vocal codas, meaning he could not move further than a few inches, but he just got on with singing and then untangled the mic when convenient. This whole sequence was emblematic of his approach at the time and thereafter; nothing was going to stand his way, least of all himself.

It was also notable as to how much guitar he was playing, unlike the early Verve gigs where it was just him and his microphone. This was a man who started as a singer, taught himself the basics of song writing, then became a musician too. In comparison with the Gallaghers, who had to share the song-writing talents and the rock star presence between them, Ashcroft now had both. No wonder he was tabloid fodder.

<u>The setlist:</u>

This Is Music
Space and Time
Catching the Butterfly
Sonnet
The Rolling People
Neon Wilderness
Weeping Willow
The Drugs Don't Work
Lucky Man
Life's an Ocean
Velvet Morning
Bitter Sweet Symphony
One Day
History
Come On

In the notes for the *Urban Hymns* boxset, the band members were still effervescent when recalling the day, 'It was one of the best days of my life. It was the dream coming true and to do it at home was a beautiful thing,' (xlviii) said Simon Jones. The other Simon (Tong) states that 'it was amazing for the town to have that influx of people from outside come to celebrate a local band. Hopefully, it made the town feel very proud. It was our way of saying thank you, paying homage – giving something back. It was very special.' (xlix)

Richard Ashcroft was especially pleased with the effect the gig had on his hometown and was, as ever, thinking in bigger terms, 'it didn't feel like we were doing it for ourselves. It was done for everyone. All the people in the town, in the region – all the people who'd backed us. It gives everyone a little strut. It opens up the possibility that you might be able to inspire people to take a different path. Be creative. Try something. We weren't born into this. We'd done it in a way that hadn't followed some corporate blueprint. We made our own path. That's why it ended up being such an intense day. There was so much riding on it.' (l)

Even the normally reserved McCabe was aware of the significance of the day, although his enthusiasm was tempered, 'Haigh Hall was definitely a milestone for us. It was both a watershed, a celebration, and a bit of a painful realisation that this was a construct and that we had better take the reins if we were to steer the band in the right direction and attain any longevity.' (li)

Seemingly nothing could stop The Verve now. It was a historic and cathartic show, the culmination of the *Urban Hymns* campaign and the band's history as a whole. Those that were there still speak highly of the day, with friends and family of the band all in attendance. Everyone went away from the gig brimming with positivity. Yet it was the last time Nick McCabe would play with The Verve for nine years.

McCabe was willing to re-join The Verve during the recording of *Urban Hymns* as he had always enjoyed the process of expressing himself through and creating music.

But the grind of touring and promotion was never enjoyable to the guitarist, presumably less so now he had less to do with the bigger songs in the set. After the Haigh Hall gig, The Verve were scheduled to headline the V98 Festival in August, play another open-air gig at Slane Castle shortly afterwards, and embark on another tour of the United States. While he was happy to play the UK and Ireland shows, the American jaunt was less appealing and so in June 1998, the band put out an announcement: 'Nick McCabe, lead guitarist with The Verve, will not be touring with the band for the rest of this year. The remaining members of the band – Simon Jones, Richard Ashcroft, Pete Salisbury, and Simon Tong – will fulfil The Verve's touring commitments as a four-piece: the dates include two headlining appearances at next month's V98 Festival. McCabe's decision has been forced by the increasing stress of touring.' (lii)

McCabe was still struggling with his health and having spoken to a doctor he was advised that he was either schizophrenic or a manic depressive. Neither of which would have been aided by the rigours of a long tour and while his absence from the band was not made out to be permanent nor were there any longer-term commitments from either party as to whether or not he would re-join. In 1999, in an interview with the website *Excellent Online*, McCabe went into details of what he was going through at the time, 'I was getting acupuncture every day and had fucking bottles of vitamins in the fridge. I had a massive fever and it knocked me down for a couple of days, and that's the only time I've ever pulled a gig.' (liii) The day he left was, once again, the last time he spoke to Richard Ashcroft for several years.

To pull a lucrative tour would have been expensive and so a replacement had to be found. Simon Tong may have been able to replace McCabe in part in the studio (or not, as it turned out) but playing live was a completely different scenario. While everything seemed to be going swimmingly from the outside looking in, The Verve were still bedevilled by problems beyond their control. They had to withdraw from the Tibetan Freedom Concert and an appearance at the Roskilde festival because Simon Jones had collapsed after a show in Munich.

Having worked with Spiritualized, Kate Radley recommended steel guitarist BJ Cole to step in as McCabe's replacement. Knowing that even trying to replace McCabe's style was a fool's errand, Ashcroft sought about looking for someone who provided something unique but would still fit in with The Verve's style. BJ Cole met the criteria perfectly. A founding member of the country-rock outfit Concise, Cole had added psychedelic flourishes to their music without detracting from its core and had a strong pedigree, having worked with John Cale and Scott Walker among many others. It was quite a sight to see a man in his fifties sitting onstage (as is required for the steel guitar) alongside musicians in their twenties, but sonically it was a good fit. It had to be, as no-one wanted The Verve to split up just as they had finally delivered greatness and with a golden opportunity to break America in the light of the success of Bitter Sweet Symphony.

After landing in the States, the new grouping spent a week rehearsing with Cole (and additional percussionist Steve Sidelynk), but unfortunately, the tour seemed cursed regardless. Some gigs had to be downsized and the support act Massive Attack pulled out early on, in the belief that they were able to put on big gigs themselves. Ashcroft later commented that he felt some of the shows were not up to their usual standards. Nick McCabe later revealed that Simon Jones had told him that the band had to use samples of his experimental sounds to beef up the sound in a live setting.

The V98 and Slane Castle gigs went down well but the air of uncertainty in the light of McCabe's departure was starting to cast a cloud. Never ones to fake it, the wheels were once again starting to come off and the band could do nothing about it, other than planning their individual futures. John Squire was backstage at Slane and Simon Jones was making plans to form a new band with him, while Ashcroft himself commented to journalist Darren Taylor that, 'after Slane, it was a relief when we finished for me. I just wanted to get home after it. Get home, close the fucking door and re-evaluate and think about it and sort the situation out.' (liv)

A welcome distraction from the confusion for Ashcroft came in the form of a collaboration with UNKLE, a trip-hop collective formed by James Lavelle (head of the legendary label Mo'Wax) and DJ Shadow. Ashcroft had built up a relationship with the pair, as exemplified by Lavelle's remix of Bitter Sweet Symphony and DJ Shadow's support slot at Haigh Hall. Ashcroft provided lyrics and vocals for a track called Lonely Souls on UNKLE's debut album *Psyence Fiction,* released in August 1998. He was one of many contributors to the album, alongside Thom Yorke of Radiohead, Mike D of the Beastie Boys and Damon Gough, better known as Badly Drawn Boy.

Having been recorded a year earlier, the album demonstrated notable vision from Lavelle, coming as it did before *OK Computer*, *Urban Hymns* and well before Gough's Mercury-winning debut album *The Hour of the Bewilderbeast.* The album received mixed reviews but Ashcroft's troubled vocals on Lonely Souls were generally regarded as one of the highlights of the album, as well as being the first piece of work Richard Ashcroft had released without The Verve. It was a glimpse into what life would be like without having to compromise with his bandmates. Meanwhile, the Bitter Sweet Symphony saga took another turn as the song was nominated for a Grammy Award in 1999's Best Song category. In another kick in the teeth, the award honoured songwriters and as such nominated Mick Jagger and Keith Richards but not Richard Ashcroft.

A year on from the stunning double success of The Drugs Don't Work and *Urban Hymns*, the future of The Verve was once again in doubt. Fan websites were rife with rumours that the band had split and in November, news leaked that Richard Ashcroft was working on a solo album. After another six months of silence, on 28 April 1999, The Verve released a formal statement on their future. The reasons were vague, but the outcome was clear: 'The decision to split the band did not come without a great deal of distress to me personally,' said Ashcroft. 'I have always given everything to the band and would have continued to do so if the circumstances had not made it impossible. I would like to thank fans for their loyal support and their phenomenal response to *Urban Hymns*. I feel more positive now a decision has been made – being in limbo isn't good for the soul. I can now move forward and put my energies into new songs for a new album.' (lv)

In an additional statement, Simon Jones confirmed that 'The remainder of the band – myself, Nick McCabe, Simon Tong – are continuing to work on our projects, while Pete Salisbury is currently working on Richard's new album. The rest of the band might even work with each other in the future. If this happens, it won't be as The Verve.' (lvi)

Where previously Nick McCabe was kicked out and partially ostracized, this time it was apparent that Richard Ashcroft was making the move to fully go solo, with McCabe on good terms with the remainder for the band. In essence, with Simon Tong unlikely to have much input in the grander scheme of things, Pete Salisbury going on to work with Ashcroft as he ventured solo and McCabe out of the picture with no plans to return, it was effectively a termination of the working relationship between the singer and Simon Jones.

Yet Jones kept the party line in coordination with his colleagues and went on to contribute music to a movie adaptation of Iain Banks' book *Complicity* with McCabe.

The erstwhile guitarist would also later disclose that Virgin were insisting that The Verve honour their contract and deliver two further albums, at the same time informing them that nothing would be released before Ashcroft's solo album.

CHAPTER SEVEN
'I Hope I See You on the Other Side of this Changing World' (2000-06)

'Imagine being the guy that's written an album on his own, bottles it near the end, feels like there's unfinished business, rings Nick McCabe up who adds some guitars, puts it out as The Verve and the same problems arise again. Imagine being that mug. I've now got to rewrite history. Everyone thinks those songs are associated with a bunch of people that I'm not with now.' (lvii)

So said Richard Ashcroft in an interview with Dorian Lynskey for *The Big Issue* before the release of his second solo album in 2002, giving a clear insight into his take on the last few years. He did have a point, *Urban Hymns* was largely his album but recorded by his former band. One would assume that Ashcroft's issues with Nick McCabe had re-emerged, but he spoke well of his former bandmate, divulging to journalist Michael Odell that, 'we had more in common at the end of the band than with any of the others. He's one of the most talented musicians I'll ever work with. An incredible artist and a beautiful person. Nick is the last person in that band I've got bad vibes with.' (lviii) Which must have made Pete Salisbury feel anxious, given that he was continuing to work with the singer.

Otherwise, Ashcroft was careful not to speak ill of his former band when launching his solo career, (for which a deal worth £10 million with Virgin and Hut was struck), instead focussing on the present and future which immediately consisted of his debut solo album, *Alone with Everybody*. The first single selected was a leftover from his writing splurge while in Bath, A Song for The Lovers, which never made it beyond the demo stage during The Verve days. The track was not a huge departure to the common man (and given Ashcroft's distinctive vocal, it was never going to be) but was different enough, a driving string epic reportedly based on Love Will Tear Us Apart by Joy Division.

The money that was being thrown Ashcroft's way by Virgin was immediately apparent in the track, which sounded cleaner, clearer, and therefore more expensive. In the video, he was required to do a slither of acting, and it featured Ashcroft walking around a hotel room and singing along to himself as the backing track. In case you weren't paying attention or didn't know, Richard Ashcroft was now very much a one-man show. The video was refreshingly un-po-faced, as the music is paused for a period as Ashcroft searches his hotel room, the tension building until proceedings recommence as he takes to the urinal to have a pee.

Backed by two new songs, (Could Be) A Country Thing, City Thing, Blues Thing and Precious Stone, the single peaked at number 3 in the UK Singles chart on its first week of release, which would have no doubt pleased his paymasters as well as the man himself. If he were lacking any confidence that he would be able to strike out on his own, his fears were allayed.

Ashcroft returned to a very different UK music scene, with rock sliding out of fashion as pop, under the guise of garage, had reclaimed the throne. The Verve's peers were scattered; even though Oasis had released an album earlier in 2000, their line-up had changed by two-fifths. Radiohead were hidden away working on a pair of albums that would test their new-found audience and Suede were one album away from splitting up. The newer breed of bands finding success all owed *Urban Hymns* a great debt; in 1999 Glaswegian outfit Travis had broken into the mainstream with *The Man Who,* a set of mournful but uplifting tracks, and a group of four young men who had met in London were about to release an album that would define the year. Coldplay's *Parachutes* was released after *Alone with Everybody,* but they had set their stall out with lead singles Shiver and Yellow.

For Ashcroft, a new venture required a new team of musicians. As well as sustaining the services of Pete Salisbury on drums and BJ Cole on slide guitar, he drafted in Chuck Leavell, formerly of the Allman Brothers and regular session musician with The Rolling Stones, Eric Clapton, and The Black Crowes, among others. On bass, he turned to Pino Palladino, who had worked with Pink Floyd and Jeff Beck and would go on to become The Who's bassist following the death of John Entwistle in 2002. His wife Kate was on keyboards, while Will Malone and Chris Potter's services were also retained on strings and production, respectively.

By this point, Chris Potter was firmly entrenched as Richard Ashcroft's right-hand man in the vein of George Martin and would continue to work with him up until 2018. Every artist needs a collaborator in some form, and it is telling that Ashcroft's singular vision only had room for a producer, rather than a song-writing partner or musician.

Recorded in London across two studios (Metropolitan and Olympic), *Alone with Everybody* oozes contentment, and when looking at where its creator was, it's not hard to see why. With the profits from *Urban Hymns* Ashcroft had been able to purchase a large mansion in the countryside (Gloucestershire) and had impending parenthood to manage; he and Kate Radley were preparing for the birth of their first child, Sonny, born three days after the album was completed. The heady days of rock & roll debauchery behind him, Ashcroft was settling down into middle age contentment ahead of society's schedule (aged 28) but completely. In preparation for the birth, he undertook his promotional duties for the album a few months before its release (rather than in the weeks before) which his record company, aware that they had a seven-million album selling songwriter to keep happy, acquiesced to.

Immediately before its release, a second single was lifted from Ashcroft's debut which, for those expecting a re-tread of *Urban Hymns*, came as a big surprise. Money to Burn was a slice of honky-tonk Elvis Presley gospel rock with a dominant brass section but with lyrics that demonstrated quite how distant Ashcroft was from his people, almost flaunting that he had 'money to burn, I'm gonna burn it on you,' following his success. The theme of contentment and pure love continued but it was not to everyone's tastes, as the single made number 17 in the charts with the accompanying video depicting Ashcroft extolling the virtues of love in the streets of New York, to largely uninterested passers-by. Frustratingly, the B-side Leave Me High was one of the better songs of this era and a place should have been found for it on the parent album. While across the Atlantic, Ashcroft road-tested some of his new tracks in a series of 'secret', stripped-down shows.

With his status as millionaire rock star set in stone, Ashcroft was able to dictate the terms of promoting the album and only participated in a handful of interviews (and shows) but when he did, the subject of The Verve inevitably (and understandably) came up. He was dignified but ambiguous when he spoke to *Chart Magazine* about the possibility of reuniting with his band-mates once again, 'You can't rule anything out as far as relationships with people. But you shared 10 years with the guys, and you've been through so much, and they're doing things that you perhaps aren't into and you're doing the same. It's all the same old differences. I think what you do is you let yourselves all go off and just let life happen. If anyone wants to force the issue, someone will, but no one's been forcing the issue that I've known about for the last 18 months. No-one's tried to get in touch with me.

'It's up to them if they want to talk about me – personally or vindictively – which I can't imagine they'd ever do, that's their choice. But it would be great to step forward without having that kind of spiteful angst that so many other people seem to carry. I think we did achieve something. We took it we put a full stop on the end of it. It was the right decision.' (lxi)

Alone with Everybody (a title pilfered from a Charles Bukowski poem) was released on 26 June 2000 and went straight in at number 1. The UK album chart for that week was a strong representation of the music scene in 2000, Ashcroft keeping rapper Eminem (*The Marshall Mathers LP*), former dance-music producer turned solo act Moby (*Play*) and wobble-headed singer/songwriter David Gray (*White Ladder*) at bay. Each of those albums would be multiple gold-selling albums and all were ubiquitous throughout the year.

If he intended to push himself even further into the mainstream (or equally, to distance himself from The Verve), then Ashcroft succeeded. Nick McCabe later went on to refer to *Urban Hymns* as a Bon Jovi album, so it would be interesting to hear his thoughts on *Alone with Everybody*. No longer channelling Funkadelic or Can, Ashcroft was now harnessing the sounds of Van Morrison, Al Green and The Band, without compromising the vast scale of the music and the universal themes. It is a very unchallenging record (not to say that is a bad thing) and as a tribute to the power of love, it is infallible.

I Get My Beat features a choir and has a sublime, prodding melody which evokes Burt Bacharach, while the equally grandiose and smooth Brave New World is the closest thing to his former band on the record, in that it changes gear midway through to a more aggressive stance that is crying out for Nick McCabe's ethereal machinations. The fried gonzo rock of New York gets the blood pumping (at a leisurely pace) with a stinging guitar and a swampy, grinding timbre. The mantra of 'are you tuning in?' acts as a chorus and eats its way into one's ears.

The tempo slows right down again for You on My Mind in My Sleep, which has a real epic beauty, but the style, lyrical content and vibe would become a template to which Ashcroft would frequently return. As the first of its kind though, it is a tender moving paean to his wife (yep, he's still deeply in love) as BJ Cole's steel guitar is given real prominence. Crazy World has moments of excellence, with a genuinely thrilling chorus that would work well as a James Bond theme, but is hampered by some textbook lyrics ('you've got that spirit, please stick with it/this world wouldn't be a world without you in it').

As he had learned on *Urban Hymns*, Richard Ashcroft's voice was an instrument of its own and he used it to great effect on the tranquil On a Beach, multi-layering the track with harmonies and different lyrics. Similarly, on the languid Slow Was My Heart, Ashcroft's delivery is the standout feature in an otherwise tepid but pleasant twinkling country ballad, while on closing track Everybody the Messaging ('everybody's got to feel the weight of death sometimes') outweighs the music, which was yet more mid-paced Americana.

For this writer, the standout track is the joyfully uplifting C'Mon People (We're Making It Now), which borrows a melody on the verse from the equally positive Reach Out (I'll Be There) by The Four Tops. While it's about love (again) it has a deftness of touch and a sense of joy that is missing from the rest of the tracks, so it was no surprise when it was selected as the third and final single. Sadly, it failed to break the top 20 (coming in number 21) when it should be one of Richard Ashcroft's signature songs. However, we should all be relieved that his idea of re-recording it in 2006 to accompany England's attempt to win the 2006 World Cup never came to fruition. As if to hammer home the point, the cover artwork of the album was a close-up of Richard Ashcroft's face, almost rectifying what he felt were his mistakes in spreading his songs across a band format.

It would be churlish to snipe at anyone's contentment, let alone someone who had the past experiences of Richard Ashcroft and indeed arguably deserved his happiness, but for long-term fans of The Verve *Alone with Everybody* was an unusual listen. There is nothing that connects it to *A Storm in Heaven*, for instance, bar the presence of Ashcroft. Not that he was going to apologise, and nor should he have had to, it was his life after all. However, that didn't stop the press from attacking it and it surely came as no surprise that it met a lukewarm reception, with various outlets describing it as 'bland' or 'gloopy' (although *The Sun* loved it). Once again, the music press could not get a handle on him, but it made little difference, as the album gained two significant accolades in hitting the number 1 slot and gaining a Mercury nomination.

Not that he was completely devoid of problems. Shortly after the album's release, Jazz Summers issued a writ against Ashcroft, which claimed that the singer telephoned Summers to inform him that his services were no longer required on the day after Summers had issued his invoice for his commission when brokering Ashcroft's solo album deal. This could have been put down to Ashcroft's ego, but during the same period, Nick McCabe was scathing about their former manager so one can presume there were issues beyond finances.

Although he would eventually embark on a UK tour at the end of 2000 and played a series of international shows in America, Japan and Europe, Ashcroft's biggest show was a headline performance at the double-headed V Festival. Wearing a T-shirt bearing the legend 'Who the Fuck Is Mick Jagger?', the set consisted mainly of solo work along with six of his compositions while with The Verve.

The setlist:

Brave New World
The Drugs Don't Work
Space and Time
A Song for The Lovers
I Get My Beat
Sonnet
C'Mon People (We're Making It Now)
On A Beach
Lucky Man
You on My Mind in My Sleep
Money to Burn
New York
History
Bitter Sweet Symphony

The lack of any group compositions came as no surprise when factoring in Ashcroft's belief that The Verve was largely a separate thing, and his band would not be able to do justice to the likes of This is Music or Come On. It was also a reminder of what he had achieved within the band off his own back. Later in the year, Ashcroft was an unlikely support act for Queen of Pop Madonna, performing a four-song set including Lonely Soul with James Lavelle and DJ Shadow at Brixton Academy.

While the singer and Pete Salisbury were building on their former band's success, the other four members of The Verve were laying low. Nick McCabe largely went to ground for the first few years of the 21st-century music-wise, contributing to a few soundtracks including *La Prochaine Fois* in 2001. The following year, he revealed in a lengthy interview with Ajay Sharma for his *Excellent Online* website that he was still working with Simon Jones, and he took the opportunity to set the record straight on a few matters. On the current state of play with the former band, he said, 'It's all just a big quandary, really, because Richard signed a "leaving member" clause, and we're still The Verve. We're still together as The Verve. But he (Ashcroft) signed the leaving (contract) and has gone solo on Virgin.

'He's obviously golden boy, so they're talking about this performance that me and Si are doing, saying, "You know, I don't think we're gonna want to put out anything before Richard does his records." I can see them sort of delaying stuff. Get the Richard Ashcroft record out. That could be four years from now or that could be never, and then maybe they'll think about putting our stuff out.' (lxii)

To muddy the waters further, Pete Salisbury was also still contracted to deliver an album to Virgin with McCabe and Jones, despite working with Ashcroft (Simon Tong, who would go on to work with Jones, was not included in the contract), and Virgin were keen that their contracts were fulfilled.

In the same interview McCabe also gave his thoughts on Ashcroft's rationality when recording *Urban Hymns*, '(Richard)'s got this record here and he thinks it's a big stadium record and it's got to be weirder, get the weird bloke back in. You know, he made all those funny noises and people will think we're crazy and experimental.

'So he gets me back and it's some sort of convoluted attempt to inject a bit of creditability in it. Then it's a really weird drugs record instead of a Robbie Williams record. Maybe I'm being a bit hard on the man. But then the record came out and he got all these accolades and slaps on the back and he's like, 'Well, what was I worrying about?" In the same interview McCabe spoke ill of Jazz Summers ('he's a fucking seedy bastard') and referred to his overall fallout of the band, 'I'm disappointed about Richard because he was once my friend. I've lost a friend and he's lost all his friends. He's got no mates. Really, no mates. Si Jones fucking, like, saved his life a couple of times. I'm not talking suicide or anything, he's just bailed him out of loads of shit through his life and he's been treated really shadowy.' (lxiii)

Meanwhile, Simon Jones busied himself with a new project. In late 1999, a classified advert in the *NME* outlined a requirement for a singer and a drummer for 'John Squire's Skunk Works Project', and it was soon disclosed that Jones was working with the former Stone Roses guitarist. After his first band dissolved, Squire had gone to find some success (after flirting with The Verve) with The Seahorses, who had a trio of hits with Love Is the Law, Blinded by The Sun and a track co-written with Liam Gallagher, called Love Me and Leave Me, in 1997. Two years later, he had parted company with singer Chris Helme and so, with the Seahorses' drummer Mark Heaney and a new, unknown singer called Duncan Baxter, he and Jones put together a new band.

However, after eight months of working together, the project fell apart and Squire retreated to his first love of painting. Undeterred, the quartet formed another band with Baxter, an additional guitarist called Dan MacBean and Jones' old friend Simon Tong called The Shining. The band enlisted Youth's assistance to produce and release an album, *True Skies*, in 2002. In an interview with Roger Morton for the *NME*, Jones was as scathing as McCabe, in his own way, about their former band, 'What I can say is that The Verve were going off in a direction of strings and ballads, and that's not where I was coming from at all. Loud guitars is it for me, and that's where I've got back to.' (lxiv)

True Skies will not go down as a lost classic but in this modern world of picking and choosing which tracks to listen to, rather than experiencing the album in one (which, in fairness could also be applied at the time by just pressing skip) there is much to enjoy. In particular, the slow, hypnotic siren running through I Wonder How and the superb opening track, the rollicking Quicksilver, all popping funk, sliding riff and BIG drums. A classic example of opening track as a statement of intent but sadly nothing else on the album comes close to its glory.

It may seem predictable, but it is also undeniable that Duncan Baxter easily draws a comparison to Richard Ashcroft, by virtue of his singing. Not in the actual sound of his voice but rather in his choices of delivery and tone. Danger is dragged down by terrace anthem 'nah nah nah's and Find A Reason could be a lost cut from a certain poodle rocker who has been named a few times recently in this text. Simon Jones's bass keeps everything together and he gets a chance to shine on I Am the One, but otherwise, it has the same intensity as The Verve but minus the songs.

The Shining burnt out quite quickly in 2003 and with little acclaim or fanfare, their output stalled at just one album. Simon Tong was swiftly snapped up by Blur who, in light of Graham Coxon being asked to leave, had a vacancy for a guitarist to play on their forthcoming *Think Tank* tour. It was the start of a fruitful relationship between Tong and Damon Albarn.

In 2002 Richard Ashcroft also returned to the music scene, firstly in collaboration with The Chemical Brothers for a track called The Test, taken from their fourth album *Come with Us.* A pounding psychedelic rumination on life ('did I pass the acid test?'), Ashcroft claimed that he had no idea what the lyrics would be until he opened his mouth in the recording booth, as he did in the early days of The Verve. Like Lonely Soul before it, it was an exciting side-step and far more cutting-edge than his early solo work. At the time he revealed he was working with innovator of drum and bass and Mercury Award-winning (for his 1999 album *OK*) Talvin Singh and was hopeful to coerce DJ Shadow into contributing to his forthcoming second album.

He was unsuccessful as DJ Shadow was nowhere to be seen when *Human Conditions* was announced but it featured an impressive cast of characters, nonetheless. Singh, who had worked with Bjork and Massive Attack, contributed tablas, beats and drones to the record while Martyn Campbell of The Lightning Seeds replaced Pino Palladino (who had moved on to The Who) on bass. Pete Salisbury (fresh from a spell as the temporary drummer for Black Rebel Motorcycle Club), Kate Radley, Chuck Leavell, Steve Sidelynk, Will Malone and Chris Potter all returned but the star attraction was Brian Wilson of The Beach Boys, who contributed backing vocals and arrangement to the album's last track, Nature is the Law.

Ashcroft explained how he was able to corral a bona fide legend into contributing to journalist Thomas Beller, 'I came out of this dream and said, "Wouldn't it be great if Brian Wilson could sing on this track?" Everybody thought I was a complete twat for thinking that he would. A few days later, someone told me Brian doesn't know who I am, but he liked the song. He did it in LA when I was in London.'

In the lead-up to the release of the album, Ashcroft revealed what he had been doing on his 30th birthday, 11 September 2001. As ever looking at the bigger picture, but with an insight that sounds chilling today, he disclosed, 'I suddenly realised that the decisions that were going to be made by the administrations in America and England were not only going to affect my life, they were going to affect my son's life, and his son's as well.' (lxv)

The first single from *Human Conditions* was the spiky, eight-minute opus Check the Meaning, released on 7 October 2002. Unlike anything from the previous album, the track evoked the directionless but adventurous spirit of early work by The Verve. Meditative and at points surreal ('I'm like a fish with legs' he cries incandescently), Ashcroft harmonises with himself throughout its entire duration as the song takes its own time.

A curious choice for a single, it just missed out on a top 10 position (at 11) but would not have sat comfortably with the likes of *Pop Idol* heroes Will Young/Gareth Gates but there was familiarity to be found one place above, as Oasis sat at number 10 with their double A-side Little by Little/She Is Love.

Lavishly produced, the sessions for his second album took place once again at the Olympic and Metropolitan studios but also at Astoria (also London) and his old haunt of Real World studios. Released two weeks after the lead single on 21 October, *Human Conditions* largely stuck to the same template as *Alone with Everybody*, with a leisurely pace dictating its ten tracks and fifty-five-minute run time. Bright Lights was an attempt to up the stakes with the guitars placed high in the mix, perhaps as a reaction to the new breed of rock that was spearheaded by New Yorkers The Strokes, but rather than recreating their zip and purpose, it plods too much to excite. Paradise returns proceedings to familiar ground with luscious strings and a well-utilised trumpet providing a sense of grandeur but sequenced as it is, preceding the philosophical but glacial God in the Numbers, fails to leave much of an impression.

Man on a Mission is pure Springsteen in its subject matter (young man leaves small town) and sound with a cracking chorus, while Running Away ironically struggles to get going despite the prominence of Talvin Singh's blissed-out, spacey contributions. Lord I've Been Trying has the structure of his *Urban Hymns* songs (another leftover from the time, and aping The Drugs Don't Work), commencing with elegant strings before building to a cathartic chorus and boisterous vocals, then dropping down and starting again. Nature Is the Law is all lush strings and Brian Wilson's contribution elevates an average song.

Human Conditions is, overall, a solid album with several good tracks but it doesn't sit in the upper echelons of Ashcroft's work simply because of its ice-melting pace. It is a crying shame the upbeat, purposeful B-Sides The Miracle or Get Up Now (from the first two singles) were not included at the expense of some of the slower tracks, as it badly needs a shot in the arm. The music press thought so too, giving it mixed-to-negative reviews with *Q* drawing the time-old comparison with Oasis; '*Human Conditions* is not a musical disaster on the scale of (Oasis's 2002 album) *Heathen Chemistry.* It's just that, from Richard Ashcroft, more is expected.' (lxvi) One fan was Chris Martin of Coldplay who defended its merits, an act which apparently 'left an impression' on its creator. However, it was another commercial success, hitting number 3 in the UK album charts in its first week. (lxvii)

Two further singles followed. After swearing that he would only ever write his own symphonies after his chastening experience with Bitter Sweet Symphony, Ashcroft built Science Of Silence entirely around the strings successfully, the track being a life-affirming ode to love (again) but with drive and intent. It deserved better than its number 14 placing in January 2003. By the time of its release in April, Buy It in Bottles was evidence (if any were needed) that Richard Ashcroft was never going to write lyrics about English men in baseball caps. It was big themes and big themes only, but they could not help the track, which only made number 26.

Contentment does not exciting pop music make and, as he was not inclined to change, Richard Ashcroft was becoming less significant in chart terms. To his credit, Ashcroft was aware of this as he explained to Michael Devereaux of *Filter*, 'it's cool to be out of time. I think in this day and age, there's so much vying for your attention on a daily basis, it's kind of nice to have music you can swim in, you can float in, music that draws you in and has got more depth to it.' (lxviii)

Where Ashcroft's influence could be felt on the likes of Snow Patrol and Keane in 2004, their heartfelt grandiosity on their sleeve, Nick McCabe's influence was also starting to filter through to the latest generation of music makers. The Music, a four-piece dance-rock act from Leeds, owed much of their sound to the widescreen ambition of The Verve and McCabe especially, so Adam Nutter from the band must surely have been grateful when McCabe remixed their single The People in 2004. Looking back the other way, McCabe appeared on his hero John Martyn's album *On the Cobbles*, on which the guitar playing is intricate and distant but recognisably him. Pete Salisbury, meanwhile, set up a drumming shop in Stockport Town Centre to busy himself between working with Ashcroft.

With the chances of Virgin being able to access any more music from the various members of The Verve remote, scattered as they were across the music business (The Shining's *True Skies* was released on Zuma Recordings, part of Sony), it was time to plunder what they did have, in the form of a Best of Collection.

Compilation Album:

This Is Music: The Singles 92-98
Released: 1 November 2004; Highest Chart Placing: 15; Label: Virgin
Track Listing: This Is Music; Slide Away; Lucky Man; History; She's A Superstar (edit); On Your Own; Blue; Sonnet; All in The Mind; The Drugs Don't Work; Gravity Grave; Bitter Sweet Symphony; This Could Be My Moment; Monte Carlo
Producers: The Verve; John Leckie; Barry Clempson; Owen Morris; Paul Schroeder; Youth; Chris Potter
Lucky Man, Sonnet, The Drugs Don't Work, and This Could Be My Moment written by Richard Ashcroft.
BSS written by Jaggar/Richards, lyrics by Richard Ashcroft.

It was a good idea not to put the tracks down in chronological order and design it more as a setlist. This Is Music only really makes sense as the first track given its competition, although one senses Richard Ashcroft's hand in the sequencing. Especially as he must have allowed the use of the unreleased This Could Be My Moment, a leftover from the *Urban Hymns* sessions. The omission of the full version of She's A Superstar in place of the edited version was a disappointment (a risk you take with a Greatest Hits collection) as the shorter version fails to do justice to the song's majesty.

The compilation was released on Virgin as Hut Recordings had been discontinued a few months earlier, which may explain why the timing of the release, Virgin keen to use the assets at their disposal. The major hook was of course the unreleased tracks, but only for Verve obsessives. This Could Be My Moment reeks of cheese and if Richard Ashcroft had chosen not to revisit the track, then it is certainly not worthy of The Verve. Monte Carlo, on the other hand, was a B-side and no more, a hypnotic percussive groove with no melody but plenty of action.

Surprisingly, given that unreleased material was included and that it was designed for a mainstream audience, the compilation underperformed upon its release. Its performance was likely hampered by no promotion whatsoever and it peaked at number 15 in the UK Album Chart. (lxix) Even the cover was an unfamiliar sight to the masses, an image of a spring based on Brian Cannon's design for She's A Superstar. In fairness, it was up against some stiff competition in the lead-up to Christmas, with Best Of compilations by Robbie Williams, Travis, Ronan Keating, Tina Turner and The Bee Gees all occupying the upper end of the chart.

After keeping a relatively low-profile for a couple of years, Richard Ashcroft re-emerged to the general public in the grandest way possible; an appearance with one of the biggest bands in the world, in front of 200,000 people and a worldwide audience watching on TV.

The Live8 initiative was set up to raise awareness of the Global Call to Action Against Poverty and the UK's own *Make Poverty History* campaigns. It was a quasi-sequel to Live Aid twenty years before, but with a different intention; rather than raising money for third-world nations, Live8 hoped to convince the world leaders of Canada, France, Germany, Italy, Japan, Russia, the United Kingdom, the United States, and the European Union to either drop the debt of or increase levels of support to aid poorer nations. Ten separate concerts took place around the world.

The UK leg of the concerts took place in London's Hyde Park on 2 July 2005 with a stellar line-up. Paul McCartney and U2 opened with Sgt. Pepper's Lonely Hearts Club Band, the temptation to utilise its opening line ('it was twenty years ago today') too irresistible to ignore (the original Live Aid took place in summer 1985) while The Who, Pink Floyd then McCartney again closed the gig. In between were pop stars new and old, including Joss Stone, Stereophonics, R.E.M, Madonna, The Killers and many more. Like U2, Coldplay had a gig scheduled for the evening and so were chosen as one of the opening acts of the day. Given it was a special occasion there were a raft of duets and unlikely collaborations (Elton John and 2005 tabloid staple Pete Doherty stood out), one of which included Richard Ashcroft performing with Coldplay.

Coldplay had always been forthcoming about their influences and were determined to help bands that had influenced them. They had brought in Tim Wheeler of Ash to work on a cover of The Buzzcocks' Everybody's Happy Nowadays for a B-side and in 2004 had given a song (Gravity) to Yorkshire band Embrace, who they had supported some years previously. Covers were a regular part of their live set and they were always quick to pay due deference to their heroes.

This time they had chosen Richard Ashcroft and The Verve and asked the singer if he would appear with them at Live8 to perform a cover. There was only one track that would suit the occasion: Bitter Sweet Symphony.

Coldplay frontman Chris Martin introduced it as 'probably the best song in the world and here's the best singer in the world,' before a beaming Richard Ashcroft took to the stage. It was a faithful rendition of his signature track and no-one could argue that on a day of such importance, Bitter Sweet Symphony couldn't stand alongside One, Won't Get Fooled Again, Wish You Were Here or Get Back as one of the most recognised songs of all time. Richard Ashcroft surely deserved his place among such hallowed company.

It also served as a useful boost to Richard Ashcroft who had been laying low, perhaps stung by the ambivalent reception *Human Conditions* had received (although the birth of a second child may also have had something to do with it). The opportunity to perform on a big stage to a huge crowd was one he had not had for a few years, and perhaps ignited a fire in his belly. It wasn't a one-off either; he would later go on to join Coldplay onstage during their stadium tour later that summer in Paris for their cover of Life's an Ocean, although Ashcroft wasn't prepared to play second fiddle and directed proceedings in Paris, insisting that Guy Berryman do more on bass. Both interpretations of The Verve tracks were faithful but, no matter how good a guitarist Jonny Buckland is, he's not Nick McCabe. Ashcroft would go on to support Coldplay the following year.

A revitalised Ashcroft went back to complete work on his third solo album and signed to a new label (Parlophone) after Hut Recordings dissolved. Chris Potter and Pete Salisbury were once again required but the bass responsibilities were shared between Terry Britten (co-author of Tina Turner's What's Love Got to Do with It?), Martin Campbell, John Giblin, and Arnie Somogyl. Will Malone, who had collaborated with Ashcroft for over a decade, was not brought in and instead the strings (there's always strings) were arranged by Julien Kershaw of the London Metropolitan Orchestra. Much of the album's work took place at Britten's State of The Ark Studios in Richmond.

A comeback was on the cards, and the lead single from his third album was Break the Night with Colour, announced in late 2005. Built around a scratchy harpsichord riff, its defiance ('you think I'm giving it up? Here we go again,') and head-nodding power took it to number 3 in the UK singles chart (lxx) upon its release in January 2006. His association with Coldplay had served as a reminder of his talent to the greater public and surely aided its performance, but patronage is never enough on its own and the single stood on its own two feet and laid the groundwork for his third album; *Keys to The World*.

The album trimmed some of the fat from *Human Conditions* and was all the better for it. Opening track Why Not Nothing? is a palette-cleanser from what had gone before, a guttural rocking blast with a raspy growl from Ashcroft that represented a new sense of purpose and the fire in his gut again. He had a renewed sense of vitriol which he directed at another big target, in this case, belief systems and their proponents ('let's get some of God's squad in the dock') to which the title was a proposed solution.

The first half of the album continued the strong start with Music Is Power and the lead single before settling into familiar territory but with an added edge. Cry 'Til The Morning was, at surface-level, a typical ballad but with passionate vocals and chilling keys. Rather than using strings as per usual, Ashcroft opts to use guitars and bass to connect emotionally, unlike on the epic Why Do Lovers? where the strings are high in the mix but a rawer vocal from Ashcroft gives a standard ballad new context. The car is steered back towards the middle of the road on closing tracks Simple Song and World Keeps Turning, both of which had strong melodies (the former being another leftover from 1996) that were designed to keep the mainstream onside.

Keys to The World is probably Richard Ashcroft's strongest solo album. It's certainly the most diverse, with tender ballads, garage rockers and more experimental tracks all sitting together coherently. His style of music was very nearly in fashion again; by 2006 the garage rock revival had petered out and polished grandiose melody was prominent in the charts. Patronage by the kings of the genre could only be a good thing and Ashcroft played the hand he was dealt well. It very nearly put him back at the top of the album chart, but it had the misfortune of being released in the same week as *Whatever People Say I Am, That's What I'm Not*, the debut album by Arctic Monkeys, which surpassed Elastica's record to be the fastest-selling debut album of all time. Richard Ashcroft had to make do with number 2.

The title track ranks as one of Richard Ashcroft's best songs. Yvonne John-Lewis, lead vocalist on Zero 7's albums, supplied a near gospel loop vocal which Ashcroft built around to form the backbone of the track with added clattering drums and near-rap coda. The most intense and righteous work of his solo career to this point, it proved that he was at his best when he infused his work with gusto. His confidence and intention to push himself were further exemplified by his choice to build a song around a sample for the first time since Bitter Sweet Symphony.

Music Is Power sampled a short section from Walter Jackson's It's All Over (written by one of Ashcroft's heroes, Curtis Mayfield), the strings adding a swing to a track already preaching positivity, the title of which would go on to become his motto. First ensuring he secured the publishing rights; it was the second single to be taken from the album. Words Just Get in The Way followed, which was a step back into old habits, a saccharine-sweet love song with an admittedly better and more subtle string arrangement than ballads past. The final single was a double A-side of Why Not Nothing? and Sweet Brother Malcolm, a song inspired by the floral tributes in memory of those who had passed. It is a tender little gem, but a single it isn't.

Unfortunately, none of the singles were able to build on Break the Night with Colour's success; Music Is Power scraped into the top twenty (20), Words Just Get in The Way barely made the top 40 (40) and the double A-side failed to chart at all. The third single was surely not helped by the video which, fifteen years on, now looks like a pastiche. Ashcroft is unshaven wearing a white jacket over a shirt that bears most of his chest. Two years later, Russell Brand would adopt a similar look playing a parody of a rock star in *Forgetting Sarah Marshall,* while as the line 'when you're feeling like you're lost' is played, Ashcroft sits next to a homeless person and points his thumb in their direction. It's unintentionally hilarious as Ricky Gervais would do a similar thing for his parody track (as David Brent) Equality Street. Simpler times.

The success of the comeback was crystallised when Ashcroft played his largest-ever solo show at Manchester's Old Trafford cricket ground to 30,000 people, but of more importance to the media was an incident that occurred two days later. Walking past the Bridge Centre Youth Club in Chippenham, Wiltshire, Ashcroft peered through the window and noticed there were no musical instruments present. Struck by an overwhelming desire to help and educate, he entered the club but was stopped by a member of staff who described him as 'dishevelled and unshaven' (they don't get many rock stars in Wiltshire). Ashcroft refused to leave and eventually the police took him into custody where he was fined £80. What was most striking and disturbing about the story is that he refused to leave and could not be reasoned with, by either the staff or the police and so, after a few years in retirement the press gleefully dug out the 'Mad Richard' stories.

Otherwise, the *Keys to The World* campaign had to go down as a success with a strong performance from the album and lead single, even if the following releases did drop away. This was the position Richard Ashcroft was continually going to find himself in. Solo artists just don't have the same magic as bands, so he was never going to hit the heights that his old friends Oasis (still going strong and undergoing a critical and commercial revival after 2005's *Don't Believe the Truth*) or new friends Coldplay were capable of. So, what to do? One avenue was apparently closed. When asked about the possibility of reforming The Verve he witheringly replied, 'You're more likely to get all four Beatles on stage.'

And yet.

CHAPTER EIGHT
'I Know We're Strangers So Come On, Fill Up My Holes' (2007-08)

Rumours were rife in mid-2007 that The Verve were reforming, and no sooner did those rumours begin to catch fire at the Glastonbury Festival, than the news was confirmed two days after the festival had shut its gates and the punters were sleeping off their comedowns in their own beds. Richard Ashcroft, Simon Jones, Nick McCabe, and Pete Salisbury were playing together, a tour was announced, and the reunited quartet spoke matter-of-factly about a new album.

It all seemed so easy. For reasons largely unknown other than to himself, Richard Ashcroft had put the idea of getting their band back together to Pete Salisbury, still holding firm as Ashcroft's rock on drums. As it happened, Salisbury had been speaking to Nick McCabe about a separate project and was able to facilitate the conversation without issue. After a three-hour telephone call between the singer and the lead guitarist, McCabe passed the proposition on to Simon Jones, who agreed, and that was that.

With The Shining long defunct, Jones had distanced himself from music's front line and while McCabe had kept himself busy making music, he had only put his head above the parapet on a handful of occasions, including playing with The Nova Saints at Bristol's Ashton Court Festival in July 2006. McCabe simplified the situation to Hamish MacBain when the band were later interviewed for the *NME,* 'I think me and Si sort of arrived at the same point, mentally. We had quite a long time being angry about it. Then once you've sort of resolved a lot of things in your own mind, you kind of realise that it wasn't such a big deal in the first place. Then you think, 'God, what went on there?' All the stuff that happened since is a little bit of a nonsense really, you know?' (lxxi)

The phone calls were so productive that the next time the four band members met was at Terry Britten's State of The Ark studio. No pints, no coffee, straight in, the air cleared so they could get on with the business of making music and seeing if that unique chemistry was still there. Simon Tong was not invited but was unlikely to be available. Since The Shining, Tong had contributed to five tracks on Gorillaz's *Demon Days* album, then joined the live band, and was working once again with Damon Albarn on a collective project dubbed The Good, The Bad & The Queen (Albarn was insistent that there was no band name) along with Afrobeat legend Tony Allen and former Clash bassist Paul Simonon.

Band reunions were once an optimistic and nostalgic dream but a few years into the 21st century it was a whole new aspect of the music business. The full effects of the loss of income via streaming platforms were yet to kick in, so there was still money to be made (via iTunes) in selling records. But the public's demand to attend live shows had increased dramatically since The Verve split in 1999. Pixies, Happy Mondays, and the Police were the latest acts to have reformed by early 2007 but the next four or five years saw the numbers escalate. The Police, Happy Mondays, Led Zeppelin, Blur, Pulp, The Libertines and eventually The Stone Roses would perform to sell-out crowds across the world (bar Led Zeppelin where it was a one-night-only affair).

The lines between decades had been blurred because of the wealth of music available at the click of a button. Without having to rely on radio to curate what they heard, listeners had virtually all recorded music immediately available to them. Richard Ashcroft himself would put it best, 'nostalgia is suffocating festivals', although that comment was made some years afterwards when things were getting out of hand. Nobody knew that they needed to see Steps again.

The Verve could also back it up with new music unlike, say, The Police who simply hit the road and reaped the financial rewards of a lucrative tour (although it was said The Verve agreed a deal worth £20 million which was later denied). The first slice of new music was released exclusively on *NME*.com for a week only in October 2007 and was literally the first thing they had played together: a rough, unmastered mix of their jam session at State of The Ark studio dubbed The Thaw Sessions, a reference to the hidden track Deep Freeze on *Urban Hymns*. But that was where the similarities would end.

The fourteen-minute jam starts right in the middle of a Nick McCabe guitar noodling which immediately intrigues as to what they were doing before the record button was pressed. If there were any doubts that the band were not taking it seriously, and in it for the music, The Thaw Sessions quickly cast them aside. It is freeform and structureless, much like their earliest work, almost ignoring the previous fifteen years and starting from scratch, indicating it was truly a band together again. Pete Salisbury's drumming was particularly exciting and almost jazz in style. It felt like he was jamming and expressing himself rather than being Ashcroft's rhythmic foundation. If it was not already clear, this was a band effort, not a continuation of Richard Ashcroft's solo career.

Nick McCabe did little more than sprinkle his particular brand of stardust, but the piece was all the better for it. In texture, lack of structure and meandering, it was an instant call back to *A Storm in Heaven*, rather than anything else that followed. The chemistry that had been upset because McCabe was not present from the outset for the *Urban Hymns* tracks had been restored without missing a beat. The instant chemistry that these four men (now all in their thirties) found in the early nineties had not left them at all. Nor had the self-belief, as the track was released online unmastered and unedited. On his blog, McCabe was matter of fact when he announced The Thaw Sessions' release: 'This is what you would have heard had you been in the room with us, and you, my friends, get to hear it. Gratis. Make of that what you will.' (lxxii)

Having a blog seems relatively archaic now, given how prominent a part social media plays in promotion, but at the time the music industry was struggling to keep up with the internet. With little guidance from the industry itself, but keen to utilise the evolving relationship between user and provider, blogs were a useful outlet. Noel Gallagher, a notorious technophobe, would use his blog to clarify any misleading headlines during Oasis' final world tour in 2008/9. Simon Jones was also a proponent and teased eager fans with insights into how the rehearsal had been going, 'September was spent in Terry Britten's amazing studio in Richmond. It's brimming with vintage gear, an old E.M.I. desk (Pink Floyd – *Dark Side of The Moon* era) and billions of guitars, old analogue gear, a treasure trove of effects pedals (Nick like a kid in a toy shop!),' he explained.

'The sessions have been pretty amazing; we certainly have an embarrassment of riches where material is concerned! We will need to do a lot of listening over the next few months before we reconvene in the new year to pull it all together! Plenty of hour-long jams and killer choons! We just need to get the balance right.

'Richard will be joining us later when we've gotten the music together. Gotta say – 'twas the greatest few days playin' old tunes! Started with Life's an Ocean and gotta say it made the hairs on the back of my neck stand up! So far we got a shortlist of about 20 odd tunes to pool from for these first gigs, in no particular order we played – Make It Till Monday, Virtual World, She's A Superstar, Gravity Grave, This Is Music, A New Decade, On Your Own, History, Stormy Clouds, Life's An Ocean, A Northern Soul, All In The Mind (sounded amazing), B.S.S. (Bitter

Sweet Symphony), Drugs Don't Work, Sonnet, Lucky Man, Come One, Weeping Willow, Rolling People, Velvet Morning, Space And Time, Man Called Sun, Star Sail and new ones.' (lxxiii)

The new ones were eventually given titles and included Mona Lisa, Rather Be (both Ashcroft compositions), Judas, Appalachian Springs and Sit and Wonder, which got an airing at the autumn gigs. As part of the announcement for their return, to great surprise and no less excitement, The Verve confirmed shows for London, Blackpool, and Glasgow, which sold out instantly.

One of the more eyebrow-raising aspects of the reunion was the news that Jazz Summers had taken up management responsibilities once again, explaining to the *NME,* 'We did keep it quite quiet. A couple of months ago, Richard Ashcroft had a conversation with me and said, "You know, we made fantastic music...I think it would be fantastic if we got back together.' (lxxiv) Summers also confirmed that no decision was made until The Verve had gone back into the studio. There was a real purity about the intention that was refreshing, with Richard Ashcroft, in particular, leaving his ego at the door, understanding that The Verve was not only a special thing but an entirely separate thing (in the main) from his solo career. He had drifted further and further away from it but the allure of The Verve, as it had been back in 1997, was too powerful even for him.

The Verve kept their counsel for a few months until that *NME* interview with Hamish MacBain in October to launch the live shows. The cover feature went into a little more detail about how the reunion came about and, pleasingly, Ashcroft and McCabe were on the same page. Referencing the split, comeback and reaction, McCabe was philosophical, 'It's just a case of perspective is something you don't have at that age. It's not a soap opera. I'm not interested in making myths or debunking myths now. If other people want to do that go ahead and do it. I really don't.' To which Ashcroft immediately jumped in, 'Exactly. That's a perfect point and I reiterate that. I reiterate Nick's point exactly.'

Ashcroft was guarded about his mindset when it came to taking the plunge and kept things simple; 'I'm not really gonna go into the details 'cos I can't really remember what I was thinking at that time. It just seemed like something that happened quite quickly, then I kind of voiced it to Pete and…'

Nick: 'We ended up having a nice chat for about 3 hours on the phone, didn't we?

Richard: 'Yeah. We had a good chat together and eventually I spoke to Si, he spoke to me and that was that.'

Simon Jones, arguably The Verve's biggest fan, was more enthusiastic about the future and his bandmates; 'I feel like I've never played as well in my life and hearing Pete after such a long break, he's never played as well in his life. Richard's got some amazing tunes and for me, when I hear Nick, he plays guitar like no other person on the planet before or since. Last night, watching him play, he's got a load of tracks on guitars but the way he blends it all…. He's just he's got a pure vision before he creates. It's amazing. That first week we did was just unbelievable.' When asked how fruitful the sessions had been in terms of new music, Ashcroft was unapologetically confident, stating they had 'an embarrassment of riches.' (lxxv) To add to the celebratory mood, *Urban Hymns* was awarded *Q* Magazine's Classic Album in October and the compilation *This Is Music* was re-issued along with an accompanying DVD.

If there were any doubts internally, The Verve either shrugged them off or faced them head-on. Their first gig back was in the bearpit that is Glasgow Academy (as passionate a crowd as one could hope for, but also the most unforgiving) on 2 November 2007. Unlike their last shows which focussed heavily on material from *Urban*

Hymns, it was a career-spanning set with something for everybody, from the fair-weather fans who only knew the hits to the most dedicated who had been there from day one and a new track thrown in for good measure. As in their early days, the band walked on to the Electric Prunes' Holy Are You.

<u>The setlist:</u>

This Is Music
Sonnet
All in The Mind
Weeping Willow
Life's an Ocean
Space and Time
Sit and Wonder
Velvet Morning
Already There
Let the Damage Begin
A Northern Soul
The Drugs Don't Work
The Rolling People
Bitter Sweet Symphony
A Man Called Sun
Lucky Man
Come On

The set was tweaked as they went along with lucky punters also being treated to A New Decade, So Sister, Gravity Grave, Stormy Clouds, On Your Own, This Time and Space and Time over the six dates. During the shows and again the year afterward, Ashcroft would introduce Bitter Sweet Symphony as a 'cover of a Staple Singers' song'.

The gig went well, although Nick McCabe would later comment that how surprised he was that Ashcroft didn't socialise with the band after the shows and instead would leave straight away, with an entourage in tow. Such was the demand for tickets that before the first leg of the tour had even started, The Verve added further dates and upgraded to London's enormous O2 Arena, Glasgow's cavernous SECC and Manchester Central. Speculation began that they would headline Glastonbury the following year.

The press gushed accordingly at their live return, with Kitty Empire writing in *The Observer*, 'when McCabe isn't turning his back to the audience, bending double over his guitar to ring some deafening washes out of it, he's always glancing at Ashcroft. Jones, meanwhile, charges around like a kid on too many E numbers, mouthing Ashcroft's words. This does not seem like an icy standoff endured solely for the money.' (lxxvi) Meanwhile, the *NME*'s Anthony Thornton commented on the difference in the attitude of The Verve's frontman, 'For those who've seen Ashcroft solo, tonight is a shock of the best kind. Gone is the dead-behind-the-eyes wannabe MOR soul singer. The indie messiah in a grandad shirt stalks the stage confidently frying thousands of minds.' (lxxvii)

Phase one of the comeback was complete. Now, Ashcroft, Jones, McCabe, and Salisbury had to deliver goods in the form of (more) new music and so burrowed down for a few months to complete an album. When they re-emerged in the spring of 2008, they embarked on a short U.S. tour which included a slot high on the bill at Coachella, the biggest festival in the United States. At the shows they had a new set-closer, a disco-flecked, purposeful driving track called either Disco, Modern Times or Love Is Noise, depending on the source.

Making hay while the sun shone, The Verve hit the 2008 festival season very hard. Michael and Emily Eavis were convinced that they were indeed worthy contenders for a headline slot at Glastonbury Festival, as well as closing proceedings at T in The Park, Rock Am Ring, Pinkpop, Oxygen, the Eden Sessions, and the V

Festival. The *NME* caught up with Simon Jones backstage at T in The Pink, who was pleased with how the summer was going, 'Because of when we split up last time, we never got to play those big slots at festivals that we – and lots of other people – always thought we'd be really suited to. So, to do a whole summer of those sorts of shows is amazing.' (lxxviii)

Broadcast live on TV, the Glastonbury slot was a bravura performance by The Verve. Simon Jones had as much confrontation within him as Ashcroft, constantly beckoning to the crowd and shouting, 'come on!' whenever he could. He mouthed virtually every single lyric and was dripping with sweat down his long hair by the end, while Nick McCabe was as enigmatic as he ever was, focussing on economically playing on his instrument and not the thousands of baying punters. It was a safe set, drawing largely from *Urban Hymns*, but had flourishes; Life's an Ocean was drawn out to become full funk, with the song incorporating the iconic bassline from Rapper's Delight by the Sugarhill Gang onto the outro and, best of all was the segue from Bitter Sweet Symphony into Love Is Noise (a trick they utilised all summer), a spine-tingling transition from new to old. Of course, the arrogance to follow your best and greatest song with your next single as set-closer was entirely in keeping with their impenetrable self-belief.

The music industry was a very different beast from the one The Verve had departed in 1999. By 2008, the internet was the platform of choice for music consumers. After much debate, digital downloads were factored in when counting the performance of singles and albums and a pattern had been set that downloads would be released a week before physical formats (primarily CDs) and the total sales would then be combined. Thereafter, in 2007, the performance of ALL songs was integrated into the singles chart, e.g., a song that had been popularised by being in an advert would lead to consumers rushing to download or stream it, which would then see it rocket up the charts. One early beneficiary was Snow Patrol's Chasing Cars, which immediately returned to the top 10, six months after its initial release.

Also, as they had done to guitar music, Radiohead had revolutionised the music industry in 2007 with the release of their seventh album *In Rainbows*. Leaked album releases, namely an album appearing online weeks before its official release date, had plagued the music industry for a decade with the implication that it would affect the commercial performance of an album. Thom Yorke and co faced the challenge head-on by adopting a new model. With ten days' notice, guitarist Jonny Greenwood announced the album's release on a 'pay-what-you-want' model. It was down to the user to decide the value of the art, with a minimum price of 0p.

This act gave power to the recording artist (temporarily) and massively destabilised the record labels. When their reunion was confirmed and new music was on the way, Jazz Summers negotiated a deal with EMI to release The Verve's fourth album. But when EMI started to make concerning comments about their marketing budget, *The Daily Telegraph* reported that, along with Robbie Williams and Coldplay, The Verve were threatening to withhold the album until they received certain assurances. The album was initially pencilled in for a June release to coincide with their headline slot at Glastonbury Festival but was pushed back to August until the issues were resolved. However, June did see the first airplay of their brand new single.

Single 13:

Love is Noise
Released: 11 August 2008; UK Chart Position: No. 4;
Label: Parlophone; Album: *Forth*
B-Sides: Chic Dub

7" single: Let the Damage Begin (Live); A Man Called Sun (Live)
Producer: Chris Potter and The Verve
Love is Noise written by The Verve/Richard Ashcroft

No-one knew what to expect with The Verve's return single (apart from the thousands of people who saw it performed live over the summer). Would it be the sonic maelstrom Verve of This Is Music? The psychedelic cowboys of Gravity Grave? The string-drenched emotions of The Drugs Don't Work? Something more in line with Richard Ashcroft's recent output?

As it turned out, it was none of the above and something completely(ish) new. Derived from another track on the forthcoming album (Columbo), Ashcroft had created a new loop (the incandescent 'woo-hoo/ah-ha' that runs throughout) on a vocoder and added it to the music which then evolved into its own thing. Extracting the section, the band gave it their full attention. With its propulsive rhythm, chiming, glistening guitar, and heavenly noises, it perhaps wasn't what the listener was expecting but was, for this fan, extremely glad to receive it. It's structured like a pop single but near electronica in style, complete with 'drop' before the last righteous chorus.

Lyrically it revels in melancholia and defiance, although Ashcroft once again reworks a William Blake poem ('And did those feet in ancient times/walk upon England's mountain green' becomes 'will those feet in modern times/walk on soles that are made in China?') adding a cynical sneer at consumerism's place in the modern world in the process alongside references to 'bright prosaic malls.'

When it eventually peaked at number 4 in the UK singles chart, Love Is Noise sat uncomfortably with Katy Perry, Kid Rock and Rihanna (lxvix) but The Verve were only ever in familiar company when they dominated the indie charts back in the early 1990s. The single stayed in the top 10 for five weeks in total and was their third top-5 single. The week after its first airplay on the radio (23 June 2008) The Verve released a free download via their website. The track in question was Mover, which finally saw the light of day fourteen years after it was first attempted during the *A Northern Soul* sessions.

It is perhaps a stretch to say it was worth the wait. It has got the devil in it, a mid-paced wall-of-sound garage rock track, but it does carry the air of the band almost being too eager to get it out of their hair. In the old days, it would have been a B-side. The actual B-side to Love Is Noise, Chic Dub, features spiky guitars which give way to a dub-heavy rhythm section to form a lengthy jam with which Richard Ashcroft occasionally joins in.

Accompanying all this was the announcement of the new album, wittily titled *Forth*. A few weeks later, it was rumoured that Richard Ashcroft would continue to play solo sets and release music by himself in conjunction with The Verve (a fact later confirmed by Ashcroft and Simon Jones) and that his first solo set for two years would be on the day of *Forth*'s release (25 August 2008) at The Last Days of Summer festival in Buckingham, which included a rare outing for See You in The Next One (Have A Good Time).

Album 4:

Forth
Released: 25 August 2008; UK Chart Placing: 1; Label: EMI/Parlophone
Track Listing: Sit and Wonder; Love Is Noise; Rather Be; Judas; Numbness; I See Houses; Noise Epic; Valium Skies; Columbo; Appalachian Springs
Producers: Chris Potter and The Verve

Rather Be, I See Houses, Valium Skies and Appalachian Springs written by Richard Ashcroft. Love Is Noise written by The Verve/Ashcroft

Recent history has not been kind to The Verve's fourth album, which seems unfair. It lacks the individuality of their previous three efforts and is more of an even balance between Ashcroft songs and band compositions, both of which have their highs and lows. The brooding, anxious Sit and Wonder crackles with electricity as an opener, with Nick McCabe choosing to adopt four or five different guitar styles over its seven-minute run time, amid clattering drums and stuttering bass from the gleeful rhythm section. Ashcroft notably opts to engage in darker, more sombre lyrical territory (as he did on the lead single) in comparison to his solo work, as if knowing that the music demands it. A splendid opener that was worth its place in the live set.

In contrast, Judas is as light as a feather with some real elegance and lump-in-the-throat moments. Its sparkling, sultry opening lures you in and while it may be bereft of a chorus or hook (not that this was a new practice for The Verve), it's dazzling at points. Following on, we get a volte-face in terms of attitude in Numbness, a snarling rocker with Simon Jones revelling in the opportunity to jam. It's bluesy but rigid and perhaps overstays its welcome with its lethargic pace, but to hear such experienced musicians baring their teeth is always welcome.

Noise Epic sounds like just the sort of flippant, short-term title that Nick McCabe would assign to a piece of music and which would have rankled with Richard Ashcroft in days gone by. As it is, it is extremely well-titled as it moves through the gears in its eight minutes until we get some frantic garage rock for the last two. Columbo follows a similar pattern, as Jones' bass wobbles and throbs while McCabe seems hell-bent on splitting the listener's ears before going as far as he can in the other direction while Ashcroft covers the full range of pitches in his vocals. A full-band jam, it is interesting to listen in the knowledge that Love Is Noise was spawned from it and trying to pick out the sequence in question enriches the listening experience.

The remaining tracks are all Richard Ashcroft compositions, but if you did not already know that and had a keen ear, it wouldn't be difficult to tell. I See Houses is very much in line with his solo work, with a traditional song structure that gives him the chance to spread his vocal wings. Valium Skies is similar in melody and intent but the presence of his three childhood friends elevates it to become a mini-epic, with some big cymbals from Salisbury and double-tracked vocals adding to the grandiosity, while Appalachian Springs (presumably a homage to classical composer Aaron Copland's *Appalachian Spring*) is equally wide-screen and windswept but also pensive at points. As a finale for the album (and for the band), it's fittingly ambitious, going big then gradually twinkling as it fades out.

The LP and Japanese versions came with an amended tracklist and two additional songs. Ma Ma Soul features a Tibetan-monk baritone as McCabe goes full free form against a whole slew of background noises, while Muhammad Ali is a funky, psychedelic strut with another chubby bass from Simon Jones. It is a shame that neither were included on the standard version of the album as, while they may drag it out, their placing (both before Appalachian Springs) breaks up the pattern of Ashcroft/Verve compositions during the second half.

There were also a handful of tracks that were leaked online during the same period; Mona Lisa was once a contender for the first single but fell from grace quickly. Another Ashcroft composition, it's the electric country-rock he had mastered during his solo career but with more edge (as supplied by his bandmates), especially on McCabe's fried solo. Blue Pacific Ocean was listed as a demo and is a shimmering, elegant track in the vein of the more fragile work on *A Storm in Heaven* but with a more confident and domineering vocal. They may have tied up a loose end in the form of Mover but in the process left a new one dangling.

Uniting with Chris Potter once more, *Forth* is a healthy balance between the sonic experimentation that The Verve excelled at and the more-straight-forward songcraft that Ashcroft brought to the table, which dominated *Urban Hymns*. The singer's compositions are easier to spot because they are united by stronger melodies whereas the rest of the tracks are more about the vibe, feel and soundscapes. Unfortunately, for that reason, it suffers against its three predecessors but there is much to enjoy with something for fans of all eras of the band.

The reviews were largely positive (albeit not overwhelmingly so); Maddy Costa from *The Guardian* highlighted McCabe's contribution as the standout feature, declaring it was his 'self-possessed musicianship that makes *Forth* worth hearing. He is consumed by the alchemist's belief that such base materials as guitars and amps can be transformed into gold,' (lxxx) while Paul Stokes of the *NME* called *Forth* 'probably the most solid foundation this quartet have had in 15 years.' (lxxxi)

The Verve's official last live appearance (barring a few TV slots) was at the V Festival in August 2008.

<u>The setlist:</u>

This Is Music
Sonnet
Space and Time
Sit and Wonder
History
Life's an Ocean

Rather Be
The Rolling People
The Drugs Don't Work
Lucky Man
Bitter Sweet Symphony
Love Is Noise

With a hit single and a series of high-profile festival slots (many of which were shown on TV, further expanding the audience), including a rain-sodden double-header at the V festival under their belt, it was surely no surprise that *Forth* went straight in at number 1 on the UK Album chart, sweeping the likes of Slipknot, The Script and Michael Jackson aside. (lxxxii) All objectives achieved.

As part of the promotion for the album, the four members of The Verve took part in a lengthy, track-by-track interview with Steve Lamacq where the air of band democracy was palpable. Jones and McCabe praised Richard Ashcroft's contributions and equally, Ashcroft went into detail about his reluctance to submit Appalachian Springs but was convinced by McCabe's enthusiasm for the song. The singer also gave his view on where The Verve sat in the modern world and what the future held, 'We've made this record and we're going to play some gigs and, you know, in a way we're almost approaching it in a much clearer way, I think, and a way that can keep the name of The Verve alive because another motivation was (that) I couldn't quite get in my head why on earth The Verve should be considered to be something that isn't alive when the songs live every day on the radio still.'

'If we want to make a record in five years, we'll make it. If we don't, we won't but we'll never, I hope, condemn the band to a sort of elephant's graveyard of rock n roll.' (lxxxiii) Around the same time, Simon Jones gave an interview to *Billboard.com* and was optimistic, 'This definitely is an ongoing concern; it's not something that we're all just gonna chuck away again. Looking back, I don't think we had to be so blunt and said, "Alright, we're splitting up!" really. We should've just chilled out for a bit and taken some time out, to be honest. But obviously, we all had a deep yearning inside to get back to do this or it wouldn't have happened. I just hope we don't split up again, now ... 'cos it becomes a bit silly, doesn't it?' (lxxxiv)

The positivity did come with some caveats from Richard Ashcroft's perspective, as he told *USA Today,* 'I don't want to invest all my mental and spiritual resources into something that may not work out. I have a family now, I do what I do, and I go home. I'm very lucky to have had the career I've had. I'm so grateful. The true friends and fans will continue to follow us faithfully. I will always continue to make music, whether it's with The Verve or on my own.' (lxxxv) Some other warning signs were beginning to emerge; with no reason given, The Verve cancelled an appearance on *Later with Jools Holland* in early September, and Simon Jones revealed in an interview with *WENN* that the band had opted not to sign a multi-album deal with EMI through fear of once again not being able to fulfil the commitment.

The official second single lifted from *Forth* was Rather Be, the remaining Ashcroft composition not mentioned above. Quite a prosaic track, it is Ashcroft-by-numbers and although it was cited as the Bitter Sweet Symphony of the pack during the initial sessions in 2007, it is a far cry from it, apart from its use of topsy-turvy, repetitive strings, plodding rather than inspiring. The video, directed by Ashcroft, doesn't even feature the rest of the band and the whole thing screams 'solo'. Accompanied across the various formats by a remix of Love Is Noise, uninspired rocker All Night Long and the strangled guitar jam Major Force as its B-sides (both of which were recorded in September 2008) the single peaked at a very disappointing number 56 in the UK charts in November.

Single 14:

Rather Be
Released: 17 November 2008; UK Chart Position: 56;
Label: Parlophone; Album: *Forth*
B-sides: Love Is Noise (Tom Middleton remix)
7" single: Major Force; All Night Long
Producer: Chris Potter and The Verve
Rather Be written by Richard Ashcroft. Love Is Noise written by The Verve/Richard Ashcroft

The single's release was the last activity by The Verve for the remainder of 2008 and in early 2009 they remained quiet, even when nominated at the Brit Awards for Best Live Act. Rumours began swirling around that once again The Verve had split up and the news was finally confirmed by *The Daily Mirror* in August 2009, "As far as Nick and Simon are concerned The Verve no longer exists," a source close to the lads tells me. "They think Richard was just using the reunion as a vehicle to get his solo career on track."

It seemed the V Festival had finished them off for a second time. The report went on to claim that the split was due to 'Nick's wild partying' (anyone with even a cursory knowledge of the band would know that was unlikely), claiming that 'their management called Simon and Nick in for a crisis meeting in September. They were told that Richard refused to tour or work with them again as long as Nick continued to drink. He quickly cleaned up his act.' (lxxxvi) As The Verve were notoriously un-media friendly, it's notable that the article contradicts itself in the space of a few sentences.

Richard Ashcroft kept a relatively low profile for the remainder of the year, stepping only briefly into the public eye for a live performance of Holy Are You, The

Verve's old entrance music, at a gig by its composer (David Axelrod) at London's Festival Hall. In early December he released one-off single The Journey, the title track for a film designed to highlight the plight of sex-trafficking with all proceeds from the track going to the Helen Bamber Foundation, a human rights organisation aimed at rebuilding the lives of victims.

After announcing that he and Jones had embarked on a new project called The Black Ships with Goldfrapp violinist Davide Rossi, McCabe would later confirm (of a fashion) the split while wryly referencing the *Daily Mirror* article on his MySpace page, 'The Verve seems to be on holiday and shows no sign of not being on holiday. I've been hesitant to breach Official-Secrets-style policy with any missives from the, well, from any front, basically. Don't ask me anything about the big V. Just let me enjoy my non-alcoholic Piña Colada.' (lxxxvii) Amusingly the article also referenced Oasis, questioning that if they could keep it together, why couldn't The Verve? Oasis split up three weeks later. God bless the British press.

CHAPTER NINE
'Jump Into the End of What You Knew. Take a Breath and Leave Yourself Behind You' (2009-17)

Some of the reports detailing The Verve's split speculated (or heard from 'a source') that Richard Ashcroft had only used their reunion as a launchpad to reignite his solo career. Whether or not that was the case, their suspicions were surely confirmed in mid-2010 when Ashcroft announced his next project. Reports in late 2009 claimed that Ashcroft had begun collaborating with American hip-hop producer No I.D. under the name United Nations of Sound. It was an unexpected move (although Ashcroft had always talked about his love of hip-hop) as No I.D. had a track record that included Kanye West, Bow Wow and G-Unit, artists not known for their love of guitars.

The *NME* reported in January 2010 that the forthcoming album would be called *Redemption* (lxxxviii) which, although later proved to be untrue, provided a curious insight into Richard Ashcroft's mindset. The first fruits of his and No I.D.'s labour was unveiled at the same time; a string-drenched, jangling confrontational track called Are You Ready. Confusingly, although the track received its first airplay in January, it was not made available online or physically and disappeared again for another few months, finally receiving a release as limited edition 12" vinyl on 12th April. Dipping his toe in sampling once again, the track was built around a string section lifted from the Bee Gees' On Time, a B-side to their 1972 single My World. The lyrics hinted at a proposed rebirth from an unspecified torment ('I've spent a season in hell') and the song features an outrageous, full-on wig-out guitar solo as its outro.

When the album was announced it had a new name (also the name of the project), *United Nations of Sound,* although in truth it was more of a pseudonym than a new band. The band was made up of Steve Wyreman on guitar, Dwayne 'DW' Wright on bass and Rico Petrillo on keyboards and samples. Benjamin Wright provided string arrangements and Chris Potter was once again recruited, this time on mixing duties, with No I.D. on production.

Notable by his absence was Pete Salisbury who, for the first time since 1991, was not required to work with Richard Ashcroft. Sadly, for the former Verve drummer, it seemed he was caught in the crossfire of whatever happened when the band split up. Salisbury was replaced first by Derrick Wright and then by Qyu Jackson, although he did not stay idle for long, shortly drafted in as a temporary replacement for The Charlatans' Jon Brookes who was forced to undergo treatment for a brain tumour. Tragically, Brookes passed away because of the tumour in 2013, and Salisbury, while never officially in the band, continues to play with The Charlatans to this day (2021).

United Nations of Sound was announced for the end of March but was pushed back until July. To keep fans on-side, they were offered the chance to sign up to a new fan club called the *RPA* (Ashcroft's initials) *Club*, a bonus of which was a further new track called Third Eye. When the album was eventually released, the band name had undergone another change, now going by the moniker of RPA & The United Nations of Sound.

On promotion duties for the album, talk naturally turned to The Verve. In an interview with *Shortlist* magazine, Ashcroft finally broke his silence but further intrigued fans, 'I can't see any reason why, after headlining Glastonbury, headlining Coachella, headlining in Japan and making an album that's better than 99 per cent of other bands' albums, The Verve would come back together. [Our 2008 reunion] was more reassuring for our audience than a nice tidy situation. The personalities are who we are, so shit happens.' The more things change….

Later in the same interview, the dichotomy at the heart of this new band was laid bare, 'You see albums coming out now and there are 15 different people on it. It's Top Trumps music – 'I'm going to Top Trump you with how many guests I've got.' (lxxxix) So, RPA & The United Nations of Sound was both a band and a solo project.

When it did see a release in June 2010 (alongside a single release of Born Again on the same day) it was largely met with derision or confusion. In *The Guardian*, Kitty Empire praised the Ashcroft's intent to spread his wings and the production levels ultimately decided that the 'expensive studio gloss holds Ashcroft back instead of lifting him' (xc) while Ash O'Keefe of *The Quietus* was even more scathing, 'as the work of a man who once declared he could fly, *United Nations of Sound* can only be considered a crash landing.' (xlc) John Roberts of the BBC was a bit kinder, 'It might not always succeed in its style-swapping, but *United Nations of Sound* is certainly as bold a record as Ashcroft's ever made.' (xci)

United Nations of Sound certainly isn't short of ambition but lacks ideas. Kudos to Ashcroft for overhauling his approach and the team behind him, but the album sadly falls short. One can see what he is attempting to do, namely put a modern spin on black American music of all genres, from soul to blues to hip-hop. The track America (giving a hint as to the target market) is underlined with some heavy beats and industrial intent and How Deep Is Your Man goes even further, punctuating the lyrics with stop-start guitars and electronic percussion (with a sample from John Lee Hooker's Boom Boom) in the most obvious attempt at the blues.

Meanwhile, This Thing Called Life does little more than add some percussion to a standard Ashcroft quasi-ballad (except about his belief, rather than his wife).

Beatitudes is as cringeworthy as one would expect from such a title and he even quotes himself ('I'm like a fish with legs'). Self-referencing would become a running theme in Richard Ashcroft's career from this point, with the bonus tracks including a song called Captain Rock, a reference to the nickname Noel Gallagher christened him with many years previously.

The experimentation is welcome as Ashcroft fully embraced the tricks he had picked up over the years, most obviously building tracks around a sample. As well as Are You Ready and How Deep Is Your Man, Ashcroft took a chord progression from The Velvet Underground's Sweet Jane for the track Royal Highness and a fragment of David Axelrod's The School Boy on which he built Life Can Be So Beautiful.

The other standout feature of the album is its thematic reference points, namely a higher power. Glory is as religious as it sounds, Life Can Be So Beautiful (complete with grating falsetto) likewise and Let My Soul Rest is just too overwrought. Drenched in strings, it is like Ashcroft can see the angels surrounding him. On This Thing Called Life he namechecks Jesus Christ and the powerful ballad, Good Lovin', is all positive vibes but little else.

For all the fresh faces and new sounds, *United Nations of Sound* largely comes across as A N Other Richard Ashcroft album and most worryingly, a sub-par effort. While this period found Richard Ashcroft at arguably his lowest ebb (sonically), there were some diamonds in the rough, specifically a fan-exclusive track called Screw You Screw Me which evoked the menace of old (i.e., The Verve) rather than the recent attempts at pop/hip-hop. Built around a loop of an UNKLE-style bassline, it was a frustrating glimpse at what could have been.

The album was released on 19 July 2010 and scraped into the top 20 (20) one week later, but soon disappeared from the UK Album Chart. Its comparatively poor performance was not Ashcroft's only concern; at the Splendour in The Grass Festival in Woodford, Australia, he stormed off stage after only one song. He reportedly kicked over his mic stand and threw a tambourine at the drum kit before walking off and advising fans that he was going to watch the Pixies.

The tantrum was linked to his apparent unhappiness at being placed opposite the American alternative rockers and also homecoming heroes Empire of The Sun, and the subsequent small crowd tipped him over the edge. Jazz Summers, back managing Ashcroft, clarified that his voice was not up to the performance due to over-use, and was advised to recuperate for 72 hours.

Unusually, Richard Ashcroft barely performed in his home nation with just a handful of UK gigs across the whole campaign, barring a special gig at the intimate Union Chapel in Islington.

Otherwise, he mainly engaged in promotional activities on both sides of the Atlantic. Ashcroft later divulged that he had suffered from pneumonia in 2010 which explains his relative inaction. But he did participate in a benefit gig following the earthquake off the coast of Tohuku in Japan, which caused a tsunami that killed over 15,000 people with countless other injuries and longer-term consequences.

The gig at Brixton Academy had been coordinated by one Liam Gallagher, shortly after the release of Beady Eye's debut album *Different Gear, Still Speeding*. After his brother had departed before an Oasis gig in Paris, causing the band to finally split up, Liam, Andy Bell, Gem Archer and Chris Sharrock had immediately rebranded themselves and continued to work. The novelty and excitement of something new had given Beady Eye the momentum with a solid, if unspectacular, debut album and Liam was able to call in some favours to put together a formidable indie-rock line-up (to a certain type of fan) which consisted of scouse trippers The Coral, a satisfied Graham Coxon (still glowing from the spectacular Blur reunion shows two years previously), Paul Weller, Stereophonics' Kelly Jones, Primal Scream and surprise guest Richard Ashcroft, with a three-song solo set, before Liam and co closed out the show. It was a healthy reminder that stripped of production and whittled down to just guitar and voice, Richard Ashcroft may be at his most powerful. Lucky Man seemed to take on a new meaning considering the occasion, and Ashcroft was visibly moved.

After signing with Razor & Tie, an American label and publishing company, a concerted effort was made to push *United Nations of Sound* to the US market for its release in March 2011, with Ashcroft hitting the promotion circuit hard. He also worked with Academy Award-winning songwriter Tom Newman on a new song (Future's Bright) for the soundtrack of *The Adjustment Bureau* starring Matt Damon and Emily Blunt. It was unfortunately to no avail and with no significant breakthrough with the project, and shortly after he turned 40, Richard Ashcroft's release schedule dried up for what turned out to be the longest time in his adult life.

Meanwhile, Nick McCabe and Simon Jones were taking their time over The Black Ships project. Violinist Davide Rossi, who played on *Forth* and featured in The Verve's live line-up, joined as did Mig Schillace. The Portishead drummer had collaborated with McCabe on a short-lived project called Field Theory and was officially announced as a member. The quartet released an EP entitled *The Kurofune* in spring 2011, a piece of work that is at various points avant-garde, ambient and industrial, broken down into sections broadly a 25-minute opus.

Speaking with *Drowned in Sound* McCabe offered, with the benefit of a few years' hindsight, some thoughts on The Verve's comeback, 'I'm a little bit disappointed in the reception *Forth* got, but I can understand why, it did go off course towards the end. It's the typical story you get from bands when they are signed to major labels, certain aspects of control get usurped. I thought I was making another kind of record.' In the same piece, he later revealed that, 'during that period though, Si and myself were pretty prolific. We had played together not as The Verve, just a year earlier, just the two of us working on new material. So, we had reacquainted with what we could do, and we are to all intents and purposes a team, Si, and myself.

'I had already forged that relationship with Mig and then when Dav got on board it was like, "Oh, wow, look at this!" It was serendipity, we ended up with four people with different personalities and different backgrounds, but we all clicked musically, with a rampant passion for playing again. It was always difficult with The Verve because it seemed that it got to the point that rehearsals were reduced to a functional preparation.' (xcii) In a striking case of deja vu, Black Ships were forced to change their name to Black Submarine after a dispute with an American electronic duo who had trademarked the name before McCabe and co. had the chance. The new collective group released a cover of Talk Talk's Renee and, with seemingly new vigour, McCabe also released rehearsal footage of some time he and Jeff Wootton, a collaborator with Gorillaz, Beady Eye, Noel Gallagher, Massive Attack and Brian Eno, had spent together jamming.

Without label pressure, Black Submarines took their time to release a debut album, but *New Shores* saw the light of day in February 2014. Having spent much of 2011 and 2012 preparing the groundwork (including having three songs on the soundtrack to a Mickey Rourke movie called *Java Heat*) the group had a logistical problem; having chosen to work with a variety of different singers to ensure their sound was as diverse as possible, it soon became apparent that coordinating live shows would be difficult. They eventually settled on a permanent vocalist in the form of Amelia Tucker.

Released through AWAL and Kobalt Music, recorded in Denmark and Chester and entirely self-funded, *New Shores* is the sound of musicians at peace with themselves. From the pumping, acid-soaked industrial electro of Black Submarine to the finger-picked acoustic Move Me Like A Mountain, it covers a broad range of musical styles with aplomb. Here So Rain empowers Nick McCabe to channel his progressive inclinations, being a marching rock beast before settling into something calmer, while the divine, cleansing Heart First aims for hitherto unexplored emotional realms.

The emotive power is not all down to McCabe's work; the track Lover also pulls at the heartstrings at the midpoint with a subline string sequence of Rossi's. It is a sprawling but patient album that unveils new secrets after each listen and musically is the next step on from *Forth*'s more tender moments, such as Judas. *New Shores* is wonderfully moving at parts and essential listening for fans of The Verve's more experimental musings.

Although Richard Ashcroft had been largely indifferent when discussing The Verve since 2009, McCabe was more grateful for the experience when he spoke to *Manchester Evening News*, '(The reunion) was a bit of a triumph over adversity. We realised all the bullshit didn't have to affect us. I don't think The Verve ever played as well as we did on that tour, but it's not to be underestimated the politics in that band; even the people who worked with us got sucked into the dysfunction.' McCabe also revealed that Pete Salisbury had opted not to contribute to Black Submarine, 'Pete Salisbury was going to come on board with us, but his loyalty to Richard and the politics... Rather than getting embroiled in that, he just bowed out gracefully.' (xciii)

As had always been the case, answers as to what happened in The Verve would slowly unveil themselves over time so the fans could get a broad picture. But McCabe also gave fans some hope when he spoke to *The*

Daily Star, 'I don't see why I couldn't work with Richard again. Richard's very black and white, and I accept that's his way of doing things. He's a good soul with a lot of good qualities, so I can never rule out doing more with him.' (xciv) Unfortunately for McCabe, the financial implications of self-funding the Black Submarine album had taken their toll and he was forced into selling some of his equipment including guitars, amps and effects pedals to finance taking a Master's degree which led to a new venture: lecturing Music Technology to students at Staffordshire University.

As mentioned, Richard Ashcroft kept a low profile in the early part of the new decade but did appear occasionally at festivals, including Hop Farm Festival in 2012 where he told *XFM* he hoped the recording of his next album would be 'a quick process'. The same year he also disclosed that he was working with Pete Salisbury once again. The following year, with no album forthcoming, he performed at Latitude Festival and made headlines when he declared to Lauren Laverne of BBC 6Music that, with no hint of irony, 'nostalgia is suffocating festivals.' The headline was misleading, as Laverne had broached the question of The Verve reforming and Ashcroft responded by attempting to motivate the newer breed of artists.

In the same interview, it appeared that Ashcroft was stung by the indifferent response to *United Nations of Sound* but defended it, 'The great thing about the United Nations of Sound album is that because it wasn't something written by Damon Albarn, it wasn't front-page news or anything. None of my followers are sheep, nobody has been told to follow Richard Ashcroft since *Urban Hymns* came out. Richard Ashcroft has never been in fashion.' (xcv) He once again confirmed that he was hoping to release new music in September of 2013.

After watching his show at Latitude, a former teacher at The Verve's alma mater, Winstanley College, was inspired to unveil a recording of a track by a pre-Verve Richard Ashcroft and Nick McCabe when they were going under the moniker Rain Garden. (xcvi) Tom Sherrington's find, Documentary is a surprisingly polished, jangly indie tune that sounds very much of its time but also showcases the strength of Ashcroft's voice at even that young age, while also demonstrating that McCabe, while not yet finding his style, was able to moderate his guitar-playing to suit the song from day one.

In August 2015, The Verve's manager Jazz Summers sadly passed away. Richard Ashcroft reportedly performed at Summers's funeral and Nick McCabe was moved enough to release a candid statement which acknowledged that, although he had 'an abrasive personality', the guitarist owed him a deb, 'Personally I have a chequered history with Jazz. We hadn't always seen eye to eye, but we reached an accord some time ago. He helped me through a particularly dark time and for that, I will always be grateful. In the last few years, I've come to understand his motivations and machinations as being fundamentally good-hearted if sometimes taking issue with the deployment.' (xcvii)

Ashcroft performed only three festival slots in 2015 but also broke cover to reveal that, finally, he had completed work on his fifth solo album. A photograph was released of his band rehearsing and consequently unveiled the new live line-up; Adam Phillips on guitar, Anthony Gorry on keys, former Ocean Colour Scene member Damon Minchella on bass and Steve Sidelnky on drums once again, with Pete Salisbury still nowhere to be seen. Ashcroft's new manager, Steve Kutner, shared a picture of a mastered album on Instagram.

The first single was announced in February 2016 (This Is How It Feels) and Richard Ashcroft came out swinging. In the press release accompanying the announcement, he disclosed that the forthcoming album would concern, 'some personal and world events (taking) a dark turn leading to a sense of urgency and a clearing of the mind.' (xcviii) The world had moved on, to an arguably darker place, a fact that Richard Ashcroft was well aware of.

The Arab Spring of 2011 was part of a series of anti-authority rebellions that went broadly worked under the slogan 'ash-sha'b yurīd isqāṭ an-niẓām ('the people want to bring down the regime'). Spreading from Tunisia to Syria, Yemen, Egypt, Libya and Bahrain, tyrannical rulers were deposed, and street demonstrations took place across the region, with social media heralded as the driving force for the message and action. The hope of revolution was soon stymied by counter-revolutionary movements, foreign state actors and destructive wars in many of the regions.

Elsewhere, the long-lasting implications of the financial crisis of 2008 were starting to take effect in the West. 2016 is now regarded as a turning point in Western democracy, as the political shock of the UK's vote to leave the European Union in June, coupled with the election of TV star and businessman Donald Trump to President of the United States in November were signposts of a new wave of populism that liberals had not seen coming. The narrative was painted as 'the people fighting back' whereas, within the political sphere, opportunistic men had seen where the wind was blowing and threw themselves into inciting 'the people' to rebel against 'the elite' and targeting immigrants as the cause of their woes since 2008.

In 2010, Richard Ashcroft's last opportunity to speak out in song, the ripples of the 2008 crisis were still in effect but by 2016 the world was a different place, and he promised his forthcoming album would be covering the important topics (still, as ever, focusing on the universal themes). In an interview with the *NME* (by now, because of a drop in the sales of print media, a free weekly) to launch the album (confirmed as *These People*) Ashcroft displayed an uncanny level of foresight, 'Whether it's something to do with Syria or Ukraine, we, the people of this country, are being treated like fools. We no longer believe in the political process. We don't believe in Punch & Judy democracy. I don't believe in a left/right paradigm. I'm no activist – it's not a political record – but scratch the surface of some of the stories presented as facts over the last few years and you come to the conclusion that we're being played on a big level.' (xcviv) Four months later, the result of the EU referendum, clouded as it is in doubt over the manipulation of information that was being cascaded to the population, would arguably prove him right. Ashcroft would later go on to decry the modern reliance on the mobile phone and revealing that he had lived without one for years as he felt like 'a slave' to his own.

That was still to come though, with the immediate focus on This Is How It Feels. Anyone hoping for a total departure from his trademark sound would have been disappointed; a string-led, grand in scale ballad with a melody that sticks in the head, the song had simplistic lyrics that could have been construed as some sort of apology (perhaps to Kate?). It was safe ground but a welcome return nonetheless, especially in the knowledge that there was some experimentation to come. Unfortunately, it didn't get anywhere near the UK Singles Chart, but for artists of his generation, this was by now par for the course.

The single format of old was all but dead by 2016. On announcing a new album, the common practice was (and is) to put the album up on streaming sites to 'pre-save' with one or more tracks immediately available to listen to. The lead track is treated as a single, with a video and radio airplay, and sometimes they may also release a 'B-side' or a bonus track. Sometimes they don't. As the later releases from *These People* would demonstrate, it's not an exact science.

Ashcroft would disclose during promotion for the album that his long hiatus was necessary and, although he did not admit it, the impression he gave was that he was chastened by the reaction to *United Nations of Sound* and it was a conscious effort to take his time over what followed. Better to collect songs and consider them, rather than rushing out a bunch of songs every 2/3 years.

The second 'single' from *These People* was released in May 2016. Hold On was seemingly a compassionate call to arms to both activists ('tear gas and pepper spray/the water cannon's on the way') and to himself ('apocalyptic mind/she soothes me with her soul') to keep on fighting the good fight. The strings were still present but given focus by a driving piano snappy, near electronic percussion. Very much a pop single but also instantly one of his best solo tracks, complete with an uplifting melody. It too failed to make a dent in the charts, but it deserved better.

In terms of music industry backing, the video highlighted the new position Ashcroft found himself in. Both Hold On and This Is How It Feels were based around the singer playing and singing to the camera in one studio but wearing 2/3 different outfits and varying the camera shots, accompanied by a handful of props. With cropped hair and the focus entirely on him, they must have been laborious shoots. Kudos to Ashcroft, a natural performer, as he does his best to keep them interesting, even going to the lengths of using his acoustic guitar to mime the string riff on This Is How It Feels.

But the videos do betray a lack of budget (remedied, oddly, by the later videos for the album) which was likely a result of Ashcroft having set up his label, Righteous Phonographic Association (note the initials) through Cooking Vinyl, an independent label in their own right (although distribution was handing by Harvest, part of Capitol records). After years on a major, Richard Ashcroft was 'indie' again.

The 'people' of the title were, according to Ashcroft, those that meant to divide society and were complicit (or active) in silencing majorities and those that were looking to erode free speech by suppressing the arts. Given the ongoing debates in 2021, Richard Ashcroft was, not for the first time, ahead of his time rather than outside of it. Although the grandiose title track broadly touched on this ('these people sent to test us/sent to play with our minds') it was wrapped in more Will Malone (brought back into the fold after fourteen years) orchestrated luscious strings.

Elsewhere, the themes were more prevalent; the stuttering electronica Everybody Needs Somebody to Hurt ('it seems') is a comment on the divisive nature of debate and opener Out Of My Body implores mankind not to trust their elected officials for fear of reprisals ('don't go looking for your Watergate/they'll destroy you') referring to whistle-blowers who would find themselves incarcerated. Elsewhere the closing tracks, the vocoder-driven Ain't The Future So Bright and the pulsing Songs of Experience seem to be intended as lessons or advice to someone, perhaps his by-now teenage children.

Picture of You is a stark acoustic track that stands apart from the rest of the album through minimal production, while They Don't Own Me manages to be both socio-political and personal. The latter was perhaps evidence that Ashcroft was still paying too much attention to his critics while thumbing his nose at them at the same time while aiming for as a big and layered a sound as possible. With Chris Potter back in the producer's chair, *These People* was his most diverse album to date. The new approach works best on Out of My Body, which starts with a distant voice and acoustic before bursting into life with a descending house beat and pointed strings. It feels like a lost dance/pop classic from the 1990s.

Taken as a whole, Ashcroft had taken the best elements of the United Nations of Sound experience, addled his bruised and grizzled voice (a consequence of age) and harnessed it into a collection of songs which he seemed to slave over. A real return to form. Richard Ashcroft was aiming for the top, with declarations of becoming the UK's biggest solo star. He dressed for the part too, the artwork for *These People* and many of the videos featured the singer in a smart light blue suit, (along with a WWII gas mask, which would become part of his ongoing image), a logical follow-on from the white trainers and polo shirts of *United Nations of Sound.* Everything was geared towards chart success, which came in the form of a number three placing on the UK album chart, six days after its release on 20 May 2016.

The *NME* was impressed, calling the album, 'both a grandmaster lesson and an antidote to the current crop of insipid singer-songwriter mulch, the sound of Ashcroft charging into the acoustic rock youth centre and showing them how it's done,' (c) although *The Observer* believed it to be, 'drowned beneath bloated production'. (ci) *Pitchfork* were satisfied overall, saying that, 'Ashcroft still has the ability to make us momentarily forget about (death),' although were dismissive of the album's 'bumper-sticker mantras.' (cii)

In an interview with *Q* magazine, on discussing The Verve Ashcroft was guarded but telling in his response, 'I wanted to make it more like Pink Floyd, where we could come back when we fancied and do something interesting. I thought some of the older wounds might have healed, and that the rest of them might have had a better perspective on their own roles in the band's demise. They allowed people to feel like my ego had broken up one of the world's biggest bands. But why would I?' (ciii)

As if to emphasis the album's success, a remarkable six tracks were lifted to perform the function of singles, whether that be getting airplay or having videos to ensure exposure across the music channels. After Hold On, They Don't Own Me followed in July, Out of My Body in October, the title track in December and Black Lines completed the set in February 2017. Another successful campaign was rounded off by some winter shows with a full 36-piece orchestra, a lavish indulgence that Ashcroft deserved.

CHAPTER TEN
'You Know There Ain't a Lot of Time, But I Know That We Can Make It' (2017-19)

With the impending twentieth anniversary of *Urban Hymns* in 2017, Universal and Virgin did not miss the opportunity to release deluxe editions of The Verve's first two albums in late 2016. The boxsets were completist to a point, but there was still a decent collection of B-sides, live outings, and demos on offer. From *A Storm in Heaven*, Brake Lights was finally given a formal release in the form of a Radio 1 Session from March 1992, as were unused session tracks Shoeshine Girl and South Pacific. Also included was a DVD of their show at Camden Town Hall from 24 years before while Brake Lights also cropped up on *A Northern Soul*, as did the original version of Mover.

The *Urban Hymns* package was not quite so generous in terms of unheard songs but included the full Haigh Hall shows on both CD and DVD. All boxsets included booklets with new interviews compiled for the occasion, some of which were quoted earlier in this book. Ashcroft did not engage in any promotion for the first two releases in 2016, leaving Nick McCabe the chance to take the interview spotlight.

Regarded as, in his eyes, his first solo album, Ashcroft did engage in the reissue of *Urban Hymns*. The pairing of Nick McCabe and Simon Jones participated in separate interviews but, frustratingly for the pair given he had been more involved in the process, Ashcroft opted not to do any promotion. Which gave Nick McCabe and Simon Jones plenty of opportunities to put things on the record.

McCabe said as much to *XS*, 'We get to redress some of the hubris and nonsense he was spouting last year about *Urban Hymns* being his first solo record and stuff like that, when we all know what we put into that record. For me, it was six months of 1997 and then I toured it to death for another year after that.'

In the same piece, McCabe revealed that Ashcroft had chosen not to release any unheard material for the reissue, which frustrated the guitarist, 'Richard said no to that, and the rest of the band were really chuffed about that particular CD.' McCabe felt that some of the unreleased material worked against the narrative that Ashcroft had built up, namely that *Urban Hymns* was entirely down to the singer and that in fact, the band were on a creative peak overall. The songs would find their way online within a year.

Of *Urban Hymns* itself, McCabe said he felt 'vindicated' that he was able to 'bring home a record that they couldn't finish with all those resources at their disposal,' (civ) and revealed that the source of the split in 1998 was a deterioration of Jones and Ashcroft's relationship but also went into detail about his own experience of the period. There was, finally, an explanation of sorts regarding the apparently final split following *Forth*, 'It went from four weeks of the band just laughing all the time to Richard disappearing. There were lots of markers that indicated that we should have maybe expected that. I just don't think that we were willing to believe that it had been reactivated for such cynical reasons but it's hard not to see it in that light now,' (cv) referring to Ashcroft's solo career.

In another interview with *xsnoize*, he mentioned that the underlying issues within the band resurfaced quite early on during the reunion, after one of their performances at the Roundhouse in London, 'Si and Richard had this almighty argument and that was it. It was the same situation that we had back in 1998. This almighty shitstorm happened and there was no coming back from that and we didn't.'

On the possibility of another reunion, McCabe revealed that Salisbury and Ashcroft had fallen out, but McCabe had approached the frontman about the possibility of working together again, 'I called Richard at his home in January 2016 to say, "Look if you wanna do it, it's ok with me, I've got some idea of how this could work." Thinking specifically about a handful of dates rather than touring commitments. I spoke to his wife for a bit and I got the feeling that he was upstairs shaking his head saying "No, no I'm not here!" (laughs) I never got the phone call back!' (cvi) When speaking with the *NME*, McCabe seemed to reveal the true reason behind The Verve's long-term issues; Ashcroft and Jones had, 'grievances that they'll never sort out.' (cvii)

Meanwhile, Pete Salisbury, now fully ensconced as The Charlatans' live drummer, surely played a part in the formation of a 'supergroup' at Tim Burgess' curated area at the Kendal Calling Festival in 2017. Aligning with The Charlatans' Martin Blunt on bass, Salisbury and McCabe rattled through instrumental versions of Super Stupid by Funkadelic, Dirt by the Stooges, Joy Division's New Dawn Fades as well as The Verve's A New Decade and Catching the Butterfly before being joined by the late, great Denise Johnson for The Rolling People. Nick McCabe would later confirm that the Black Submarines project had become too expensive to sustain, albeit without formally announcing the band's dissolution.

With Oasis finally calling it a day in 2009, Richard Ashcroft found himself in the awkward position of having to navigate a position in between the brothers without rocking any boats. He was able to do successfully for some years (in 2015 Noel Gallagher revealed he would 'love to make an album' with Ashcroft) by speaking highly of the pair when asked. However, as is the modern age and exacerbated by social media, fans took it upon themselves to pick either Liam or Noel (a ridiculous proposition). In later 2017, Noel Gallagher dragged Richard Ashcroft into the crosshairs.

During an interview with the *Sodajerker* podcast, the middle Gallagher brother was asked if he would be interested in co-writing music. Noel responded with a lengthy answer which, as he so often does, ended up ruffling a few feathers:

'I'm offended by singer/songwriters who, when you scratch the surface, actually don't do any fucking song writing. I'm offended by that. As far as I can be aware, if you scratch the surface of any fucking songwriter in this country, they've all got a team of songwriters behind them apart from me, (Paul) Weller and Johnny Marr. I'm struggling to think of anybody else. Ashcroft, our kid (Liam), all the way to fucking Ed Sheeran….and the little fella from fucking One Direction. They've all got an army of songwriters behind them.'

Quite why Gallagher had this opinion is unclear, not least because it was not true. Yes, *United Nations of Sound* (which Noel had claimed he 'loved') does feature four co-credits but that was due to the sampling rather than the structure of the song, and *These People* was listed entirely to Ashcroft. The interview didn't go unnoticed by either Noel's younger brother Liam (who posted on Twitter, 'Dig me out all day long rkid but Richard Ashcroft pisses all over you and the 2 Ronnie's every day of the week as you were LG (sic)) or by Ashcroft himself, who took the unusual step of using his Twitter account (nominally used for marketing and promotion) to query, 'I don't write my own songs? You want to qualify that NG'. He then followed it up with a screenshot of the dictionary definition of 'defamation.'

Whatever his reasons, Noel Gallagher had forced Ashcroft to pick a side and subsequently the bond between Liam Gallagher and Richard Ashcroft grew stronger, with the latter regularly supporting the former as he successfully launched a solo career, including a surprise slot at a big show in Finsbury Park in the summer of 2018.

Ashcroft's summer shows, which also included a support slot for Roger Waters in London's Hyde Park, were a precursor to his sixth album: *Natural Rebel*. The lead single, Surprised by The Joy, was released on 10 September 2018 and after his dalliance with the direct pop of the previous album, it was the most Radio 2-friendly he had ever been. Ashcroft was back to writing a country-esque ode to his wife and domestic bliss ('I wanna walk the garden with you') with added ELO-strings.

The video is sweet if cheesy, as he reunites with his wife after driving to meet her from his studio in London. Ashcroft's continuing to extol the virtues of happiness may not have been to everyone's tastes but his defiance and belief to keep doing so have to be admired.

Based on the lead single, one you would think he would play it safe from here, with anthemic acoustic indie-rock the order of the day. But tying in with the title, that proves not to be the case. The key influence on *Natural Rebel* was the late Tom Petty, who was himself anthemic but with a more middle-of-the-road hue. It was most prominent on All My Dreams, a curious choice for an album opener, the subject matter also being the love of his life. More of the same followed on Birds Fly, a full-on string ballad with a twist. As ever, Ashcroft was going for timeless song writing, always covering the big themes of love, life, and pain. From his viewpoint, doing so was a rebellious act, even if the music was less so.

There followed a lot more in this vein, including That's How Strong and We All Bleed, with its gospel-Stones vibe. The former track almost swallows itself in heartfelt sentimentality ('I don't care what they're saying/that's how strong this love is') while the latter is glacial in pace but weary in delivery. 'I'm born to sing,' he asserts, and it is undeniable that there is something about that tremendous baritone that always keeps the listener involved, specifically on the former where his voice nearly does take flight.

As was to be expected on the tenth album of his career, there were echoes to past work; That's When I Feel It harkened back to *Keys to The World*, and A Man in Motion would have sat comfortably on *Human Conditions*. Unusually, the second half is stronger and embraces new sounds in the form of 70s disco-strut of Born to Be Strangers, story-telling songcraft (Streets of Amsterdam) and, best of all, the rocking Money Money.

Even though he is a leading figure in rock and roll, Ashcroft has rarely (if ever) 'rocked' out in a traditional way. As brash as This Is Music was, it's a psychedelic ungainly wall of noise while Why Not Nothing? may be up-tempo but it was driven by acoustic guitar. Money Money sees Ashcroft attack a Stooges-esque killer riff with gusto, wrenching his voice while he makes barbed comments, perhaps on behalf of The Rolling Stones, to his old nemesis ABKCO, 'you know I'm taking back the turf from the ones who sold you out'. It is a gonzo-fried rocker, electrifying in a way Ashcroft had not been before, and goes to show that, despite the MOR sound of the rest of the album, he is capable of being vital when he wants, even after 25 years in the game, and that nothing puts a better fire in his belly than a personal wronging (or specifically that one). More of this would be welcome.

For the first time since 1997, production duties were not fulfilled by Chris Potter. Instead, two producers worked on the album (alongside himself): Jon Kelly and Emre Ramazanoglu, who had a wealth of credits between them, including Paul McCartney and Jarvis Cocker. The album was announced along with news that Ashcroft had signed to the BMG, a huge international music publisher and label, although Righteous Phonographic Association was still listed. Following Surprised by The Joy as singles were Born to Be Strangers and That's When I Feel It which once again failed to make a dent in the UK Top 40.

The album, however, was yet another top 5 success for Ashcroft, coming in at No. 4 on 25 October 2018. (cviii)

The music press didn't fail to notice quite how directly Ashcroft was embracing middle-age and the reviews were mixed. The *NME* noted that he was, 'so comfortable in his well-worn big ballad rut that he almost sounds like a pastiche of himself,' (civi) while *Drowned In Sound* went one step further and compared him, oddly, to the current crop of artists, 'In an era where the likes of Idles and Sleaford Mods (whose frontman is actually a year older than Ashcroft) are kicking up a storm against the political and social injustice that surrounds them, there's never been a less appropriate time to say nothing than the present.' (civii)

It was a similar story from the mainstream press. *The Guardian*, never Ashcroft's biggest supporters, was surprisingly positive for once, noting his progression, 'Ashcroft's gone from *A Storm in Heaven* to this. And he's good at it,' (civiii) but *The Independent* was scathing, highlighting the quality of the last song but clarifying that Money Money 'isn't worth the jaw-clenching 40 minutes, six seconds it takes to get there.' (cix)

The promotion for Natural Rebel was given an unexpected (and unwelcome) boost when Ashcroft appeared on Sky's *Soccer AM*. While sitting down on the interview sofa, an eagle-eyed viewer noticed that a small bit of paper fell out of Ashcroft's trouser leg. Inevitably the tweets wrote themselves ('looks like the drugs do work' etc. etc, chortle chortle) and cast the singer in a dim light. As we know by now, Richard Ashcroft is not one to stay silent on such challenges and took to Instagram to post a video where he clarified the situation: 'Just a quick message to a couple of you trolls on Twitter who are making a name for yourselves out of me, and also people moralising and virtue signalling. Number one: Cocaine and I have had no relationship for decades. Number two: Don't you ever surmise what has fallen out of my pocket. And don't bring my children into it. You're on thin ice. Don't libel my name. My dad didn't like litter and I don't really like litter. But it gets a bit preposterous in my pocket. In The Verve I was known as Columbo, so get your facts right. You're on thin ice. Peace.' (cx)

For an ardent fan, it was the first they had ever heard of this nickname (although a track on *Forth* was titled Columbo, so there may have been something in it) but Ashcroft doubled down on it and released a song called Hey Columbo, a two-minute acoustic track that he rattled off quickly, with lyrics which revelled in his outlaw status. Nick Power of The Coral made a parody video in response and the two went back and forth over Instagram, seemingly in good spirits.

Meanwhile, in an interview with Radio X, the subject of The Verve was brought up and, for the first time, Ashcroft acknowledged that the breakup had been messy, but he was keen to keep his counsel, 'I made a decision quite a number of years ago that I'd see how it pans out. I'll see if any other member tries to re-write history, you know? I'll see how many bizarre takes on events stack up and then maybe one I'll go; "You know what? I'll write the book.'

'If I'm attempting to make myself the saint in this, that would be wrong. But I think what has happened is, because I've kind of remained a bit silent on the subject because I don't want to burn people out publicly, I don't want to just say, "here we go this, this is what I was dealing with." I'm not that kind of guy.'

He went on to reveal, albeit subconsciously, that he was still protective of his former band and respected his old friends, 'I don't want to be responsible for messing up someone. I don't want to be responsible for that because the things that happened in The Verve, it was heavy stuff. It was real. It wasn't just frivolous nonsense, you know what I mean? There was real people's lives. It was real emotions.' He added, 'And I've never really thought about completely clarifying it because I know that damage that clarifying it will do.

'So I am prepared to take any bizarre, misshapen, fucked-up version of that reality said by anyone. Any ex-member of the band can say what the fuck they like, because I know the truth and I'm cool with it. And I know what I've done since the band, and I know what I'll continue to do. Judge me by my works.' (cxi)

CHAPTER ELEVEN
'It's A Bitter Sweet Symphony, That's Life' (2019-21)

Ashcroft's comments are not the final word on The Verve (it's doubtful there ever will be one while all the members are still alive) but it brings the story up to date. Although, if this is a story, there should be a happy ending (of sorts).

As well as supporting Liam Gallagher and Roger Waters, in the summer of 2018, Richard Ashcroft was the special guest for The Rolling Stones. It seems unlikely that our hero would have let such an opportunity to write some wrongs pass. At the very least he would have been likely to air his thoughts on the Bitter Sweet Symphony saga to its co-writers. In what would otherwise be an extraordinary coincidence, the following year Richard Ashcroft's magnum opus became solely his work.

In a public statement, he announced, 'It gives me great pleasure to announce as of last month Mick Jagger and Keith Richards agreed to give me their share of the song Bitter Sweet Symphony. This remarkable and life-affirming turn of events was made possible by a kind and magnanimous gesture from Mick and Keith, who have also agreed that they are happy for the writing credit to exclude their names and all royalties derived from the song they will now pass to me.

'I would like to thank the main players in this. My management Steve Kutner and John Kennedy, the Stones' manager Joyce Smith and Jody Klein for actually taking the call. Lastly a huge unreserved heartfelt thanks and respect to Mick and Keith. Music is power.' (cxii)

This may spectacularly backfire on his fans. A content Richard Ashcroft is all well and good, but he is at his most interesting when he has something to say, and the Bitter Sweet Symphony situation left scars which will

surely now heal. This is pure flippancy of course, it is only right that he should be the sole beneficiary of his work and to the man himself, it must be immensely satisfying after 22 years of torment. At the same time, Ashcroft received a lifetime achievement award from Ivor Novello.
Which begs the question; what next for Richard Ashcroft? If he is picking up lifetime achievement awards then, by definition, that means he should be slowing down (although receiving the award before he had even turned 50 does make the gesture a little premature) which may happen, but he will undoubtedly continue to release music.

After years of playing only his compositions, the last half-decade has seen him turn his hand to covering songs. He performed a cover of Prince's Little Red Corvette as a tribute to the man when he died in 2016, while around Christmas 2019 he released a cover of Have Yourself A Merry Little Christmas and played Santa Claus at a live session on Virgin Radio. In a separate session for the same station, he treated the listeners to a cover of Pastor L Barret's 1971 track Just Like A Ship, and in February 2021 he officially released a cover of John Lennon's Bring on The Lucie (FREDA PEEPLE) (capitalised for emphasis).

This could have been a contentious move. In 2020, as the COVID-19 pandemic swept the world, former Stone Roses frontman Ian Brown took to Twitter to decry the whole thing as a conspiracy and for people to fight the power in their actions, discouraging people from being vaccinated. Ashcroft's old friend Noel Gallagher was less revolutionary but no less controversial, revealing in an interview that he had chosen not to wear a face mask out in public. Both acts received widespread criticism.

Ashcroft's choice of cover could be construed in one of two ways. The chorus ('free the people now,') could be viewed as a reaction to the various lockdowns that nations across the world were forced to endure in response to the pandemic. Alternatively, the lyrics on the verse take oppressive governments to task in a more general way and, given the anti-authoritarian stance Ashcroft has taken in recent years (especially on *These People*), perhaps he chose Bring on The Lucie (Freda Peeple) to make a broader point.

At the time of writing, Ashcroft has two dates pencilled in for May 2021 at the London Palladium (likely to be rescheduled) and mentioned in an interview with Radio X (to celebrate Bitter Sweet Symphony winning a Best Track of the 1990s accolade) that he was re-recording his best songs for an acoustic album. This seems an odd move, especially as he could more than justify a straight-forward 'Best Of' collection after six solo albums and twenty-one years. Of course, it would not include the songs written when he was part of The Verve, which may explain the acoustic album.

A Best of or Singles collection would be formidable if it spanned his whole career. Taking only singles into account, any album that includes A Song for The Lovers, C'Mon People (We're Making It Now), Check the Meaning, Science of Silence, Break The Night With Colour, Music Is Power, Why Not Nothing? Are You Ready, Hold On, Out Of My Body and Born To Be Strangers (for example) would be welcome. It is surely only a matter of time. Whatever he does next, he is bound to take his large fanbase with him.

Simon Tong keeps himself busy. The Good, The Bad & The Queen (eventually confirmed as the name of the band) released a second album in 2018 (*Merrie Land*) and toured it extensively in 2019. The sad death of Tony Allen in 2020 means the collective is unlikely to make a third album, with the Afrobeat legend being such a key component. Tong is also a founder of The Magnetic North along with Erland Cooper. The band released two albums in 2012 and 2016.

Nick McCabe is still involved in music and pops up fairly frequently with new material. In 2018 he contributed guitar on ShadowParty's self-titled debut album, mastered another one (Sunstack Jones) and took to Bandcamp to release a 45-minute ambient piece titled We Are Are We in early 2021. McCabe claims to have over five albums' worth of material ready to go whenever he feels ready to release them, as well as sustaining his day job as a lecturer. According to McCabe, Simon Jones runs a rehearsal facility in Chester and 'likes to travel a lot' and being such a talented drummer, Pete Salisbury will presumably keep on touring with The Charlatans.

Is there is any hope for The Verve? As we have learned, anything is possible with that band, but the chances of a reunion do seem slimmer than they ever have. The death of Jazz Summers means there is no mediator available and in conjunction with Pete's 'fallout' with Richard, two avenues for a reunion (or at least a conversation) are now closed off.

With hindsight, the last reunion did have a sense of finality or, more accurately, of finishing business. When *Urban Hymns* went stratospheric, The Verve only did one big show (Haigh Hall) and a handful of festivals. In 2008 they headlined virtually all of them and released a new album to boot. It is hard to argue that they did not please everyone. Older songs such as A Man Called Sun and Already There were included in the smaller shows (for the long-term fans) and they covered huge swathes of their catalogue across the tours. The hits satisfied the newer fans, and the shows were largely well-received. It may seem flippant, but they looked good too, all still in their thirties. Not that The Verve were ever likely to be rocking in their old age like The Who or The Rolling Stones.

Their legacy is intact. Even back in the 1990s, they were influencing those around them. Chester band Mansun were openly named after A Man Called Sun (although was one of many theories regarding their name), and Yorkshire indie outfit Embrace's 1998 album, *The Good Will Out*, owed a great debt to *Urban Hymns*. In more recent times, echoes of The Verve can be heard in Snow Patrol, Exit Calm, The Music, Warpaint, Temples and The Horrors, to name but a few.

They made a solid album which (in this writer's opinion) included one of their best-ever singles, and Richard Ashcroft took a backseat when it came to the publicity, happy to let Nick McCabe and Simon Jones handle that side of things (for once). It was a full-blooded and apparently wholehearted commitment to the band, if only for a year and a half. From the outside looking in, everyone looked happy and if people were looking anxiously at the relationship between Ashcroft and McCabe to fall apart, it seems they were looking in the wrong place. It is none of our business, but it appears that Simon Jones and Richard Ashcroft have personal issues between them that have been percolating for a long time.

So, logic would dictate that The Verve are finished. But very little about that band makes sense. Why did they recruit Jazz Summers as manager in 2007, given the acrimony? Numerous other options were surely available. Why did Richard Ashcroft sack Nick McCabe in 1995 and then reinstall him a year later? We have half-answers, but each member of the band seems incredibly protective of their reputation and legacy.

Perhaps we should just appreciate what we had. Richard Ashcroft often cites The Verve's story as being pure Spinal Tap, and while that is presumably true (he did live it, after all) it is so much more than that. In a sleepy town, four friends form a band. They go on to become an awesome guitarist, a dynamic rhythm section and, eventually, a world-class singer and songwriter. They create music organically through jamming until they harness their own sound. They take over the world for a short time, along the way going through problems with drugs, and then split up in a sea of acrimony and legal battles. They reform to reclaim their place at the top of rock's table, satiating thousands of fans around the world before splitting again. Their musical legacy is four distinct albums rather than variants of the same album. It is the purest rock and roll story imaginable. They should have achieved so much more but that crystalises the legend and, more importantly, the myth.

Ultimately, whether The Verve reform or not is down to Richard Ashcroft. His attitude lends itself to the idea that he could try anything, but the song always takes priority. Sprawling ambience is not his preferred method of delivery as it is with Nick McCabe. Ashcroft cites himself as a troubadour and so perhaps sees the rest of his days as one man and a guitar, and what the audience gets now is all they are ever going to get.

But then, we have been here twice before. The third time's the charm?

THE END

ABOUT THE AUTHOR

Richard Bowes writes about music as much as he can, regularly reviewing albums and gigs and conducting interviews for Live4ever.com.

'Modern Music Masters – The Verve' is his second book. 'Some Might Say – The Definitive Story of Oasis' was published in 2020.

For more information about the Modern Music Masters series:
modernmusicmastersuk@gmail.com
www.modernmusicmasters.uk

References

(i) Quoted in Select Magazine, March 1998
(ii) Quoted from Egan, Sean 'Star Sail' pg. 25 Askill Publishing, (2017)
(iii) Quoted from Egan, Sean 'Star Sail' pg.35 Askill Publishing (2017)
(iv) Quoted from Melody Maker, 13 June 1992
(v) Quoted from Melody Maker, 13 June 1992
(vi) Quoted from Melody Maker, 13 June 1992
(vii) Quoted from Melody Maker, 13 June 1992
(cviv) Quoted in A Storm In Heaven deluxe edition, (2016). Interview by Joe Clay
(viii) Quoted in A Storm In Heaven deluxe edition, (2016). Interview by Joe Clay
(ix) Quoted in A Storm In Heaven deluxe edition, (2016). Interview by Joe Clay
(x) Quoted in Melody Maker, 15 May 1993
(xi) Quoted in Melody Maker, 15 May 1993
(xii) Quoted in Melody Maker, 15 May 1993
(xiii) Q magazine, July 1993
(xiv) Q magazine, July 1993
(xv) Q magazine, July 1993
(xvi) Quoted from Egan, Sean 'Star Sail' pg. 86 Askill Publishing (2017)
(xvii) Quoted in A Northern Soul deluxe edition, (2016). Interview by Joe Clay
(xviii) Quoted from Egan, Sean 'Star Sail' pg. 97 Askill Publishing (2017)
(xix) Quoted from Egan, Sean 'Star Sail' pg. 97 Askill Publishing (2017)
(xx) Quoted in A Northern Soul deluxe edition, (2016). Interview by Joe Clay
(xxi) Quoted in A Northern Soul deluxe edition, (2016). Interview by Joe Clay
(xxii) Quoted in A Northern Soul deluxe edition, (2016). Interview by Joe Clay
(xxiii) NME, 11 June 1994
(xxiv) Select Magazine, June 1995
(xxv) Guitar Magazine, 07/07/1995
(xxvi) Dazed and Confused Magazine, July 1995
(xxvii) Quoted from Egan, Sean 'Star Sail' pg. 122 Askill Publishing (2017)
(xxviii) Quoted from Egan, Sean 'Star Sail' pg. 132 Askill Publishing

(2017)
(xxix) https://en.wikipedia.org/wiki/List_of_best-selling_albums_in_the_United_Kingdom
(xxx) Quoted in Urban Hymns deluxe edition, (2017). Interview by Joe Clay
(xxxi) Quoted from Egan, Sean 'Star Sail' pg. 145 Askill Publishing (2017)
(xxxii) Quoted in Urban Hymns deluxe edition, (2017). Interview by Joe Clay
(xxxiii) Quoted in Urban Hymns deluxe edition, (2017). Interview by Joe Clay
(xxxiv) Quoted in Urban Hymns deluxe edition, (2017). Interview by Joe Clay

(xxxv) *"500 Greatest Songs of All Time". Rolling Stone. Retrieved 22 August 2011.^ "Bitter Sweet Symphony ranked 59th most celebrated song". Acclaimed Music. Retrieved 30 November 2020.*

(xxxvi) Quoted in Urban Hymns deluxe edition, (2017). Interview by Joe Clay
(xxxvii) Only "Official Singles Chart Top 100". Official Charts Company. Retrieved June 30, 2018.
(xxxviii) Quoted from Baker, Trevor 'Richard Ashcroft: The Verve, Burning Money & The Human Condition' pg. 114 Independent Music Press (2008)
(xxxix) https://ivorsacademy.com/awards/the-ivors/archive/?ay=1998
(xl) *British album certifications – Verve, The – Urban Hymns". British Phonographic Industry.*
(xli) https://www.officialcharts.com/artist/27816/verve/
(xlii) NME, 31st October 1997
(xliii) Rolling Stone, 16th October 1997
(xliv) https://www.stereogum.com/3604/songs_u2_wish_they_wrote/news/
(xlv) Quoted from Egan, Sean 'Star Sail' pg. 173 Askill Publishing (2017)
(xlvi) https://www.rollingstone.com/music/music-features/the-verve-richard-ashcrofts-bittersweet-triumph-241277/
(xlvii) i https://www.rollingstone.com/music/music-features/the-verve-richard-ashcrofts-bittersweet-triumph-241277/
(xvc) Quoted from Baker, Trevor 'Richard Ashcroft: The Verve,

Burning Money & The Human Condition' pg. 121 Independent Music Press (2008)
(xlviii) Quoted in Urban Hymns deluxe edition, (2017). Interview by Joe Clay
(xlix) Quoted in Urban Hymns deluxe edition, (2017). Interview by Joe Clay
(l) Quoted in Urban Hymns deluxe edition, (2017). Interview by Joe Clay
(li) Quoted in Urban Hymns deluxe edition, (2017). Interview by Joe Clay
(lii) https://www.nme.com/news/music/the-verve-69-1388492
(liii) https://web.archive.org/web/20070409002209/http://www.excellentonline.com/article.php3?story_id=786
(liv) Quoted from Baker, Trevor 'Richard Ashcroft: The Verve, Burning Money & The Human Condition' pg. 135 Independent Music Press (2008)
(lv) https://www.nme.com/news/music/the-verve-75-1390329
(lvi) https://www.nme.com/news/music/the-verve-75-1390329
(lvii) The Big Issue, 30th September 2002
(lviii) Quoted from Baker, Trevor 'Richard Ashcroft: The Verve, Burning Money & The Human Condition' pg. 139 Independent Music Press (2008)
(lxi) Chart Magazine, May 2000
(lxii) https://web.archive.org/web/20070409002209/http://www.excellentonline.com/article.php3?story_id=786
(lxiii) https://web.archive.org/web/20070409002209/http://www.excellentonline.com/article.php3?story_id=786
(lxiv) https://www.nme.com/news/music/the-verve-61-1369855
(lxv) Quoted from Baker, Trevor 'Richard Ashcroft: The Verve, Burning Money & The Human Condition' pg. 158 Independent Music Press (2008)
(lxvi) Q Magazine, November 2002
(lxvii) https://en.wikipedia.org/wiki/Human_Conditions
(lxviii) Quoted from Baker, Trevor 'Richard Ashcroft: The Verve, Burning Money & The Human Condition' pg. 164 Independent Music Press (2008)
(lxix)

https://en.wikipedia.org/wiki/This_Is_Music:_The_Singles_92%E2%80%9398
(lxx) https://www.officialcharts.com/charts/singles-chart/20060115/7501
(lxxi) NME, 7 September 2007
(lxxii) https://myspace.com/nickmccabeuk
(lxxiii) Quoted from Simon Jones's blog, 2007
(lxxiv) NME, 7 July 2007
(lxxv) NME, 3th October 2007
(lxxvi) Quoted from Baker, Trevor 'Richard Ashcroft: The Verve, Burning Money & The Human Condition' pg. 196 Independent Music Press (2008)
(lxxvii) Quoted from Baker, Trevor 'Richard Ashcroft: The Verve, Burning Money & The Human Condition' pg. 195 Independent Music Press (2008)
(lxxviii) NME 19/08/08
(lxvix) "Official Singles Chart Top 100". Official Charts Company. Retrieved 25 June 2018.
(lxxx) https://www.theguardian.com/music/2008/aug/22/rockreview.theverve
(lxxxi) https://www.nme.com/reviews/reviews-the-verve-9850-327428
(lxxxii) "British album certifications – The Verve – Forth". British Phonographic Industry.
(lxxxiii) https://www.thevervelive.com/2008/08/the-verves-forth-revealed-part-1.html#more
(lxxxiv) https://www.thevervelive.com/2008/08/verve-to-continue-on-after-forth-and.html
(lxxxv) https://www.thevervelive.com/2008/09/verve-goes-forth-and-forges-reunion.html
(lxxxvi) https://www.mirror.co.uk/3am/celebrity-news/the-gigs-dont-work--the-verve-finally-411481
(lxxxvii) https://www.mirror.co.uk/3am/celebrity-news/the-gigs-dont-work--the-verve-finally-411481
(lxxxviii) https://www.nme.com/news/music/richard-ashcroft-26-1295664
(lxxxix) https://www.thevervelive.com/2010/07/richard-ashcroft-interview-with.html
(xc) https://www.theguardian.com/music/2010/jul/18/rpa-united-nations-of-sound

(xlc) https://thequietus.com/articles/04752-richard-ashcroft-united-nations-of-sound-review
(xci) https://www.bbc.co.uk/music/reviews/z2cg/
(xcii) https://drownedinsound.com/in_depth/4142968-%E2%80%9Cthis-is-the-best-band-we%E2%80%99ve-ever-been-in-%E2%80%9D---dis-meets-nick-mccabe
(xciii) https://www.manchestereveningnews.co.uk/whats-on/music-nightlife-news/nick-mccabe-sailing-calmer-waters-6662869
(xciv) https://www.dailystar.co.uk/showbiz/nick-mccabe-wouldn-rule-out-18723225
(xcv) https://www.thevervelive.com/2012/06/richard-ashcroft-new-album-to-be-song.html
(xcvi) https://www.nme.com/news/music/the-verve-5-1255239
(xcvi) https://www.thevervelive.com/2013/07/pre-verve-track-documentary-featuring.html
(xcvii) https://www.thevervelive.com/2015/08/nick-mccabe-pays-tribute-to-jazz-summers.html
(xcviii) https://www.nme.com/news/music/richard-ashcroft-14-1198178
(xcviv) NME 25/02/16
(c) https://www.nme.com/reviews/reviews-richard-ashcroft-16476-305921#:~:text=On%20the%20surface%2C%20this%20will,media%20surreptitiously%20manipulating%20the%20masses.
(ci) https://www.theguardian.com/music/2016/may/22/richard-ashcroft-these-people-review
(cii) https://pitchfork.com/reviews/albums/21894-these-people/
(ciii) Q Magazine, June 2016
(civ) https://www.xsnoize.com/interview-the-verve-guitarist-nick-mccabe-revisits-urban-hymns-20-years-later/
(cv) https://www.xsnoize.com/interview-the-verve-guitarist-nick-mccabe-revisits-urban-hymns-20-years-later/
(cvi) https://www.xsnoize.com/interview-the-verve-guitarist-nick-mccabe-revisits-urban-hymns-20-years-later/
(cvii) https://www.nme.com/news/music/verves-nick-mccabe-discusses-urban-hymns-richard-ashcroft-oasis-2135236
(cviii) https://www.officialcharts.com/charts/albums-chart/20181026/7502/
(civi) https://www.nme.com/reviews/richard-ashcroft-natural-rebel-review-2390213
(civii)

https://drownedinsound.com/releases/20458/reviews/4152079
(civiii) https://www.theguardian.com/music/2018/oct/19/richard-ashcroft-natural-rebel-review-roots-rocking-for-car-journeys-everywhere
(cix) https://www.independent.co.uk/arts-entertainment/music/reviews/richard-ashcroft-natural-rebel-album-review-tracklist-release-date-tour-a8588916.html
(cx) https://www.nme.com/news/music/richard-ashcroft-responds-trolls-questioning-debris-fell-pocket-soccer-am-x-factor-rant-2382851
(cxi) https://www.nme.com/news/music/richard-ashcroft-silent-the-verve-split-2423466
(cxii) https://www.nme.com/news/music/rolling-stones-richard-ashcroft-share-bitter-sweet-symphony-royalties-rights-2491569

Made in the USA
Monee, IL
06 August 2021

75068116R00105